CLASSIC BUS

YEARBOOK – 8

Edited by Gavin Booth

Ian Allan

60th ANNIVERSARY

CONTENTS

First published 2002

ISBN 0 7110 2851 3

Design by Hieroglyph

Published by Ian Allan Publishing

An imprint of Ian Allan Publishing Ltd, Molesey Road, Hersham, Surrey KT12 4RG

Printed by Ian Allan Printing Ltd, Molesey Road, Hersham, Surrey KT12 4RG

Code: 0204/B2

INTRODUCTION

ANOTHER YEAR, another Yearbook. And although this is the eighth book in the series, it is the tenth anniversary year for *Classic Bus* magazine, a fact that is celebrated in these pages in the ABC of CB. What, I am often asked, *is* a Classic Bus anyway, a question I am careful not to define too exactly in case I offend readers' sensitivities. As far as the bi-monthly *Classic Bus* magazine is concerned, anything newer than 20 years old is not Classic; anything older is. Not very precise, I know, but CB readers tend to be very subjective about buses, and this prevents letters from the busman's equivalent of Disgusted of Tunbridge Wells. And if 20 years sounds very new, just think what has changed in that time, and look at the photo-feature illustrating in colour what was new and what was around in 1982.

If you thought that the Tilling Group epitomised the total standardisation approach – and it was difficult to see beyond those Bristol/ECW products that seemed to come from the Tilling sausage-machine – Michael Dryhurst's article reminds us that there were some very non-standard buses in the group's fleets, some because of takeovers, others because Bristol and ECW couldn't always provide exactly what some Tilling companies were wanting. So we find AECs, Albions, Beadles, Bedfords, a Crossley, Daimlers, Dennises, Fodens, Guys, Leylands and Maudslays.

More non-standard types feature in David Harvey's article on preselector Guy Arab III double-deckers. Somehow the idea of Guys with preselectors doesn't sit as comfortably as AECs and Daimlers, yet several operators chose this option. And were the Birmingham 'new-look' Arabs, MkIIIs or MkIVs – or something in between?

AEC and Leyland were for many years the deadliest of rivals for lucrative bus orders, yet Alan Townsin reminds us that AEC borrowed heavily from Leyland in the design of its legendary 8.8-litre diesel engine in the 1930s.

An even more obscure connection from Robert E Jowitt in 'Buses and Belfries' – not so many shapely young ladies from Robert this time as his mind (or certainly his camera) was on higher things as he considers the relationship between buses (and, yes, the inevitable tram) and ecclesiastical architecture.

Strachans was one of the best-known coachbuilders in Britain at one time, but suffered from the fluctuations of the market and changes in ownership. It survived long enough to build AEC Merlins for London Transport, and played a significant part in what we would come to deride as the 'breadvan' style of minibus. Geoff Burrows worked at Strachans for some years and presents a potted history of the company, supported by adverts and official photos.

John Aldridge regularly contributes his 'I Invited Myself' column to *Classic Bus* magazine, recounting episodes in his long journalistic career when his interest led him to a good story. In the Yearbook, John writes about Lancashire at the time he left Leyland, where he edited the *Leyland Journal*, to pursue his career in the weekly transport press.

There are three other illustrated features – one in full colour, one in black-and-white and the other using contemporary material from the 1940s. The colour feature by Ted Jones illustrates some of the fine and decidedly individual liveries that were worn by BET Group buses in the years before the group's acquisition by the state and disappearance into the newly-formed National Bus Company. Just as Tilling strove for standardisation right down to two main liveries, BET allowed its companies to do their own thing – as long as the money was coming in.

The black-and-white photo-feature by Chris Palmer illustrates an aspect of buses that rarely appears in books like this – the back-ends of buses. I regularly get calls from the diecast manufacturers looking for references for a new model or new livery, and the detail that is most difficult to research is the back end. While most photographers take front, nearside and offside shots, few take back-end shots.

David Fletcher has dipped into his collection of memorabilia from the once-great Crosville company and has come up with two goodies. One is a souvenir booklet given to passengers travelling on a Leyland Titan that had reached one million miles, and the other is a booklet gathering together the fascinating wartime newspaper adverts, a mixture of patriotic encouragement and gentle hand-slapping.

In between all of these are features from the bi-monthly *Classic Bus* magazine – like Alan Millar's Checkpoint articles providing instant knowledge on bus-related topics, and Chris Drew's Letters from London, where his drawings illustrate the different types of London bus that have shared the same type letters. Alan Millar contributes a Classic Blunderbus to each issue of the magazine, but for the Yearbook he singles out a Classic *Wonder*bus.

And Roger Davies signs off with one of his distinctive Roger and Out columns, this time recalling how he discovered variety and excitement among the buses of the north of England.

Enjoy the book, and if you don't already see the magazine, give it a try!

Gavin Booth
Edinburgh

Front cover: *A classic bus if ever there was one – the preserved 1954 Ipswich Corporation AEC Regent III with RT-like Park Royal body, no.16 (CDX 516) represents what to many is a classic combination of shapes and sounds.*
John Robinson

Page 1: *One of the delightful illustrations by* Punch *cartoonist Douglas England, used by Crosville in its wartime newspaper advertising. A selection of these adverts appears on pages 19-21.*

Back cover, upper: *Buses that to many readers are still 'modern' are increasingly being preserved and restored, like this Southport Corporation 1973 Leyland Atlantean AN68/1R with Alexander bodywork, no.89 (VWM 89L). It is now owned by the photographer.*
John Robinson

Back cover, lower: *A more unusual combination – a preserved 1958 Leyland Tiger Cub PSUC1/2 with Yeates 43-seat bodywork from the fleet of the well-regarded independent, Delaine of Bourne, no.47 (MTL 750).*
John Robinson

Although Bristol Tramways had Eastern Coach Works bodywork fitted to a batch of Leyland PD1A, there was also a number bodied by BTCC itself, like C4011, seen here after some heavy rebuilding of the upper-deck front.
All photos by Michael Dryhurst

MOST transport historians acknowledge that the London General Omnibus Company's B type double-decker was the first motorbus produced with a view to standardising on a particular type and product. Although the LGOC, and the London Passenger Transport Board and London Transport Executive after it, always strove for a wholly-standardised motorbus fleet, the goal was really never achieved. Do I hear you say 'Pooh-pooh and tosh, what about the RT family? Isn't that the ultimate standardisation of one bus type?' Well, was it? From one manufacturer came 4,825 chassis, and from another 2,131; bodywork produced by seven different companies, the products of only two being totally interchangeable without modification. Wasn't a bad try, though . . .

The Tilling Group had the same aspiration. After all, it had its own chassis-manufacturing facility via its Bristol Tramways subsidiary, which produced at its Brislington works a range of bus chassis; in addition, the group (and the 'Tilling Group' is defined here as comprising those directly-owned subsidiaries, plus the former National Omnibus & Transport Co Ltd companies and the Tilling Motor Services Ltd subsidiaries) had a body manufacturing entity, Eastern Coach Works Ltd, at Lowestoft. Both Bristol and ECW had supplied vehicles to operators outside the Tilling Group, but with nationalisation and

PIPEDRE

Standard bus in non-standard colours. When BTCC assumed control of the Cheltenham District company, the livery of the latter was retained, as worn by this Bristol KSW6B with ECW lowbridge bodywork.

custodianship of the British Transport Commission, open market sales came to an end in 1948, although some years were to pass before all such deliveries were completed. But with sales restricted now to only BTC fleets, there would appear to be the opportunity to produce a standardised bus for the group's fleets, with all of the many benefits that would flow from such a programme . . .

Nice try – shame about the acquisitions

The BTC was one of the many agencies created by the postwar Labour government, the basic manifesto of which was to nationalise anything that moved (plus a lot that didn't!). So, in addition to acquiring the Tilling Group, the BTC really was charged with acquiring all other bus companies, even municipals, if they could be persuaded to throw in their lot with the BTC, and there were grandiose plans for regional transport boards, which would meld together BTC, municipal and independent interests.

AM!

Were Tilling's aspirations to total fleet standardisation a pipedream? MICHAEL DRYHURST thinks so

Above:
Cumberland did not purchase any Bristol/ECW vehicles until 1954, the majority of the postwar intake being Leylands. Seen in Carlisle in May 1959 is no.196, a Leyland Tiger with Northern Coachbuilders bodywork.

Left: *A number of Tilling Group companies purchased the Beadle semi-chassisless bus; most of these featured Bedford running units. Eastern Counties had 16 of these vehicles, powered by Gardner 4LK engines.*

Acquisitions brought into the Eastern National fleet numerous non-standard vehicles, especially on the takeover of the City Coach Co. Seen in Brentwood is ENOC no.1218, a Daimler CVD6 with Roberts lowbridge body, which had originated with City.

The BET Group was totally against nationalisation and mounted a successful defence of its bus-operating subsidiaries, but many companies sold out to the BTC, concluding that nationalisation was inevitable or, often in the case of independents, having no-one to whom the business could be passed. Once purchased by the BTC, the acquired company was subsumed into the nearest ex-Tilling fleet, such transfer bringing with it a vehicle fleet that inevitably comprised of every permutation of body/chassis combination except that of Bristol/Eastern Coach Works . . .

Wot, no standardisation?

It cannot be said that the intent wasn't there, because it was, but nevertheless, acquisitions aside, there were some odd deliveries made to Tilling Group subsidiaries once 'standardisation' had become the official game-plan.

The Brighton, Hove & District Omnibus Co was set-up in November 1935, being the successor to the Hove-based operations of Thomas Tilling Ltd, which company had large numbers of the AEC Regent I in both its London and Sussex fleets. While BH&D took

delivery of Bristol double-deckers from 1936 onwards, it was 1956 before its motorbus fleet was 100% Bristol, although these buses were powered by AEC 7.7-litre, Bristol AVW, and Gardner 5LW or 6LW engines. But until 1959 BH&D still had 11 non-standard buses. The Brighton Transport Act of 1938 allowed for BH&D to operate a percentage of the trolleybus mileage. Bristol had built but two trolleybuses, and those in 1931. Thus in 1939 BH&D took delivery of eight AEC 661T and in 1948 followed three BUT 9611T; all were bodied by Weymann.

One would think it could be fairly safe to assume that the Bristol Tramways & Carriage Co would be well and truly wedded to Bristol chassis on which were mounted Eastern Coach Works bodies. Wrong. In 1947/8 BTCC took delivery of a large fleet of Leyland Titan PD1, and although ECW provided bodywork, a number was bodied by BTCC itself; in

Top: *When in Jowitt-land . . . Two schoolgirls walk in front of Hants & Dorset no.H1221, one of six Leyland Titan PD2/1 supplied in 1949. The side ventilators on both decks appear to be non-original while the shade over the windscreen was a standard H&D fitting, as it was with Southdown.*

Above: *ECW did not build a true coach body until 1950 (adapting its standard saloon for such work), so Tilling subsidiaries purchasing Bristol coaches had them fitted with bodywork by various companies. Hants & Dorset no.672 was a Bristol L6G with 28-seat body by Portsmouth Aviation.*

Above: *The Lincolnshire fleet received a huge intake of non-standard vehicles when it absorbed Enterprise & Silver Dawn. No.1809 was an AEC Regal O662 with Duple bus bodywork that had been subject to rebuilding. A standard Bristol L/ECW brings up the rear.*

Left: *Probably unique in a Tilling Group fleet was this Crossley SD42/7. Numbered 103 with Southern Vectis, it came with the fleet of Nash Coaches, in which operator's former premises it is seen here. The 33-seat body is by Whitson, and this 1949-built coach is now preserved.*

addition, this company also received a fleet of Bedford OB, with Duple bus bodywork. When the Red & White group sold out to the BTC, the Cheltenham District subsidiary passed to BTCC, which brought into the Bristol fleet buses of AEC, Albion and Guy manufacture.

The Caledonian Omnibus Co, although a Tilling Group company, on creation by the BTC of the Scottish Omnibuses Group was transferred to Western SMT, whence went its AEC, Albion, Dennis and Leyland vehicles, plus a handful of 'standard' Bristol/ECW K and L types.

The largest company in the group was Crosville Motor Services Ltd., which despite its size almost achieved 100% Bristol/ECW standardisation. However, as a result of a BTC dictate, CMS received a batch of Leyland Tiger PS1/1 that had originally been intended for the Balfour Beatty group, which had recently sold its bus-operating subsidiaries to the BTC. While supposedly standardising on the Bristol K double-decker, the BTC purchased from Leyland 100 Titan PD1A chassis, but did have these buses bodied by Eastern Coach Works; Crosville was a recipient of some of these lowbridge double-deckers, and later received all-Leyland PD2/1s in highbridge and lowbridge form.

If you didn't know its parentage, on encountering Cumberland Motor Services you could be forgiven of thinking this was not a BTC affiliate. Leylands predominated and bodywork came from many different companies; in fact, Leylands were received right up until 1952 and Cumberland did not receive any 'standard' Bristol/ECW buses until 1954, six years after the creation of the BTC.

The Eastern Counties Omnibus Co was strong on standardising on the Bristol/ECW product, but also it had its vehicle idiosyncrasies. Perhaps leading amongst these was the group of 1932-built Leyland Titan TD2 buses that in the postwar period were fitted with Gardner 5LW engines, CovRad radiators,

With the sale to the British Transport Commission of the Red & White group, a number of R&W subsidiaries passed to Tilling Group companies. One such was Newbury & District, the services and vehicles of which were assumed by Thames Valley. Seen here at Newbury is TV no.H10, a 1950 Guy Arab III with stylish Duple 57-seat bodywork alongside 'standard fare' nos.645 and 702, Bristol KSW6B/ECW lowbridge of 1952/3 respectively. Note that no.645 is in the revised livery while no.702 retains its two cream relief bands. A rear view of a sister Guy appears elsewhere in this book.

postwar Bristol front wings and ECW bodies, of both highbridge and lowbridge layout. These lasted until the end of the 1950s, and ECOC received 20 of the Titan PD1A/ECW buses.

On the single-deck front, ECOC took delivery of 16 Beadle/Bedford semi-chassisless buses plus a Beadle/Dennis prototype; all of these had the Gardner 4LK engine as did the 16 ECW semi-chassisless buses, which had running units from scrapped Dennis Ace vehicles. In 1954 the company received 18 Bedford OB/Duple coaches, but again powered by the 4LK; acquisition of smaller companies brought into the ECOC fleet vehicles by AEC, Albion, Dennis, Foden and Maudslay, all of which were retained and operated.

The Eastern National Omnibus Co had been purchasing Bristol/ECW products well before World War 2, but the postwar shortage of new vehicles

The other Red & White company that passed into Thames Valley control was South Midland with a large fleet of Duple-bodied AEC Regal coaches, Guy Arab LUFs and this apparent standard – which it wasn't. No.85 was an AEC Regal IV with Bristol LS-style ECW 37-seat coach body.

prompted the company to buy 'non-standard'. This included some Titan PD1A/ECW double-deckers, plus Beadle/Bedford chassisless buses and a couple of Beadle-bodied Bedford OB. But by acquisitions and secondhand purchases, the ENOC fleet became incredibly diverse. On 1 January 1950, Hicks Bros of Braintree was taken over, bringing with it Leylands of both double- and single-deck types, Guy Arab deckers and a Maudslay. The large City Coach Co had been assumed by Westcliff-on-Sea Motor Services and when the latter passed to ENOC control it brought with it Bedford, Daimler, Leyland and Seddon vehicles, in addition to some elderly AEC Regent open-toppers, that had originated with BH&D. And mopping-up of some of the Canvey Island independents saw into the fleet AEC, Albion, and Daimler utility buses. What price standardisation here?

In the postwar years, Hants & Dorset Motor Services also took in batches of very non-standard buses, plus single-deck Bristols with a variety of bodies that did not emanate from Lowestoft. Possibly the most unusual Tilling Group double-decker purchase was that of six AEC Regent III 6812A; these were an order diverted from Western SMT and carried L53R bodywork by Northern Counties. Following-on sequentially from these were half-a-dozen Leyland Titan PD2/1, with the Lancashire company's standard H56R bodies. In addition to the foregoing, H&D received seven of the 100 PD1A/ECW. On the saloon side there were seven

Bedford OB/Beadle B20F, two Beadle/Morris-Commercial B35R semi-chassisless, while the company had Bristol coach chassis with bodies by Beadle, Dutfield and Portsmouth Aviation.

The Lincolnshire Road Car Co took postwar delivery of some of the Titan PD1A/ECW and Bedford-Beadle chassisless saloons, but standardisation here was dealt a poor hand when Enterprise & Silver Dawn was acquired, which brought into the fleet many non-standard makes, particularly AEC Regal and Regent types, of various models.

Thought of often as a 'non-standard' company, the Southern Vectis double-deck fleet was very standardised. A relatively large number of Bristol/ECW buses was purchased, and wartime Bristols received new ECW bodies (together with Gardner 5LW engines); the only non-standard buses was a brace of open-toppers, ex-BH&D AEC, but even these were 5LW-powered. Like many Tilling Group companies, SVOC took delivery of the ubiquitous Bedford OB/Duple as there was not such a vehicle produced by Bristol/ECW, and later went on to

Mention is made that a number of companies and municipal fleets purchased Bristol/ECW products prior to the restriction on their sale outside BTC fleets. North Western no.171, a Bristol L5G/ECW is seen at Sheffield.

Bedford SB and VAL. Interesting acquisitions that were retained and operated were Commer Avenger/ Harrington, Crossley SD42/Whitson and Dennis Lancet lll/Duple, all of these coaches coming with the business of Nash, Ventnor.

The Thames Valley Traction Co standardised on the Bristol/ECW product from 1946 onwards, deviating only because of the weight restriction on Marlow Bridge, which prompted purchase of a Bedford OB, while 16 Bristol L6B delivered in 1949/50 had Windover coach bodies. But with the BTC purchase of the Red & White group, this put Newbury & District and South Midland under the Thames Valley wing, bringing in its wake Guy Arab III double-deckers with Duple bodywork of both highbridge and lowbridge configuration, and coaches/saloons of AEC Regal I, III, IV, Guy Arab LUF, and Leyland PS1 types, with mostly Duple bodies, but also ECW and Lydney/BBW, while a Bedford OB/ Beadle arrived in 1949.

United Automobile Services was a committed

Bristol/ECW company, and those companies it acquired, were, for various reasons, combined into a UAS subsidiary, Durham District Services; it was to this company that passed non-standard acquired vehicles, although one slipped through to UAS itself, the famous (or is it 'infamous'?) Guy Arab III/ Willowbrook double-decker, no.GGH1. Later acquisitions saw nonstandard types pass into the UAS fleet itself, such as the AEC Reliance, Bedford YRT and Leyland Leopard.

The United Counties Omnibus Co fleet was very standardised on the Bristol/ECW product, buying nothing else in the postwar period. However, in 1952 the Eastern National Beds/Bucks/Herts area passed to UCOC, and with it many former ENOC vehicles,

Top: *Looking somewhat dwarfed by a Devon General Leyland Atlantean is Western National no.2929, a Leyland PD1A with lowbridge ECW bodywork. BTC purchased 100 such buses, which were allocated to several Tilling Group companies.*

Above: *A number of Tilling Group subsidiaries purchased the ubiquitous Bedford OB, in both bus and coach forms. One of the latter is seen here, Southern National no.1448, in Royal Blue livery; this coach is now preserved.*

including 12 of the Titan PD1A/ECW double-deckers.

Did the West Yorkshire Road Car Co have anything non-standard apart from the eight Bedford OB; four Beadle buses and four Duple coaches? I think not . . .?

Associated companies Southern National and Western National also dipped into the non-standard pool. While the only double-decker deviations were 20 of the inevitable Titan PD1A/ECW, there was more interest on the saloon front, particularly with the 12 AEC Regal III 6821A, which although carrying bodies of 'Tilling' style were built not by ECW but by Strachans Successors Ltd, of London. The WNOC group also had some Beadle/Bedford chassisless buses and a large number of Bedford OB coaches; additionally, standard Bristol chassis were supplied with Beadle and Duple coach bodies. Acquisitions saw the purchase, and retention, of an AEC Regal/Harrington and a Bedford SB/Duple.

The Wilts & Dorset Motor Services Ltd was another Tilling Group company that in the postwar years standardised rigidly on the Bristol/ECW product, only to have its well-planned intake thwarted by the Red & White takeover; Basingstoke-based Venture Ltd passed to W&D, and with it a

Wilts & Dorset no.496 was one of four AEC Regal III coaches that were acquired with the fleet of Venture Ltd. Duple built the 33-seat body.

fleet of AEC Regal, Regal III, Regent III and Bedford OB. Like its neighbours Hants & Dorset and Western National, W&D purchased Bristol coaches with bodies other than by ECW, in this case by Beadle and Portsmouth Aviation.

On the other hand, despite the foregoing, the Tilling Group companies did purchase an enormous number of Bristol chassis that were bodied by Eastern Coach Works, and apart from a few variations there was also standardisation on fleet livery, destination box layout and even the moquette on the seats . . . plus the bus garages and bus stations, all of which were designed by 'Tilling' architects, to a similar 'look' and with a standard type of brick face.

I suppose today's nearest standard is the Dennis Dart SLF/TransBus Pointer – which is why we all enjoy *Classic Bus* so much! **CB**

This year's nomination deserves the award for longevity alone, suggests ALAN MILLAR

THE BEDFORD SB holds the record for being in production for longer than any other single British bus or coach model. It was launched in 1950 and continued to be built right up to the end of Bedford's existence as a General Motors brand in 1986.

Before you rush off to pen irate letters to the publisher or to the editor of *Classic Bus*, let me stop you in your tracks. Yes, I know that the Leyland Titan lasted for 42 years, even if you ignore a four-year suspension of production during World War 2. But as someone once said, about the only thing the first TD1 and the last PD3 had in common was the badge on their radiators – and even that was held on by a different type of screw. The SB of 1987 was essentially the same as the SB of 1950, just a bit bigger and powered by a diesel rather than petrol engine. Even if some crazy people inside GM had tried to make us believe we should call those later models something daft like NJM.

This was a classic design. Like many, it had been superseded by other classic designs a good few years before it ceased to be built. But the fact that Bus Éireann – the last big operator in the British Isles to buy the type – didn't finally withdraw its last SB school buses until 2001 is a sign of how widely and for how long this model was appreciated.

Bedford took a calculated risk when it launched the SB, for this was the replacement for a different sort of mass-market classic, the 29-seat, bonneted OB. The OB was the last of a 20-year line of Chevrolet and Bedford chassis designed like scaled-up motor cars. It was cosy, compact, easily manoeuvred and was simple to maintain. By taking the same approach to the coach and rural bus market as it was taking with trucks, Bedford leaped up a scale and replaced the OB with a 33-seater in which the driver sat over the front axle and beside the engine, rather than behind both of them.

The SB, you see, was the bus version of the S-type truck, just as the OB was the bus equivalent of the OL truck. The S-type benefited from GM's American approach to design, with lots of bulges, curves and a raked windscreen. The idea was that some of this would carry forward to the SB, but the first bodies produced by Duple – for long the bodybuilder with a close sales and marketing relationship with Bedford – only incorporated some of the goods vehicle's flair.

It wasn't until 1953 that Duple's original Vega body was replaced by something more adventurous and in keeping with the forward-looking vision of the new chassis. And it took until production began for the 1955 season before that design reached full maturity with a feature that gave it a nickname that befits a classic product of the end of the golden age of coaching. Its grille. The 1953 Vega had a rather plain oval grille, which was a deal more stylish than the truck-derived panel on the previous model, but the 1955 season ushered in the large, wide, divided chrome grille that caused those coaches to be known as 'butterfly front' SBs.

Let it be whispered, but there were butterfly-front Leyland Comets, Commer Avengers and indeed also some butterfly-front Bedford C4 and C5 29-seaters, but it was on the many SBs built from 1955 to 1958 that this design is most fondly remembered. It was modern without being outrageous. It stood the test of time.

During those early years, the SB also went through a series of adaptations that kept it in the forefront. By 1952 it could hold 37 seats and by 1950 it was at last being built to 30ft length with seats for 41 – a full dozen more than could be squeezed into the old OB. The transformation was as great under its bonnet, for the original six-cylinder petrol engine was joined by

The SB as it first appeared with Duple Vega bodywork. This example was working in the Scottish Borders for Atkinson, Morebattle.
Richard Iles

the option of the Perkins R6 diesel from 1953 and by Bedford's own diesel and the Leyland O.350 from 1957. The original SB became the SBG ('G' for 'gasoline' as this was an American-owned company) when the SBO ('O' for 'oil', as diesels were widely known in the 1930s) appeared in 1953. From 1957, the options were SB1 (Bedford diesel), SB3 (petrol) and SB8 (Leyland), and from 1962 the SB1 and SB8 were replaced by the bigger-engined SB5 (Bedford diesel) and SB13 (Leyland O.370).

Duple – and the lower-volume coachbuilders that competed against its market leadership – continued to keep up with the design-conscious times as the Rock'n'Roll late-1950s gave way to the Swinging Sixties. Curved glass begat the Super Vega for the 1959 season and the Bella Vega for 1963. By then, the first stirrings of obsolescence were being felt by the SB as coaches got bigger still and the mass market moved on to coaches with their entrance ahead of the front axle. Yet even then it played a part in this next stage of its evolution.

Yeates of Loughborough had managed to produce a 44-seat SB conversion in the early 1960s, with just such a layout and its own Fiesta body. The design seems to have come with its own share of problems, but it was causing sufficient stirs in the market for Bedford to develop its own VAM, which was itself derived closely from the SB and appeared in 1965.

The plan – as Alan Townsin reminds us in his *The Bedford Story* book of 1996 – was for the VAM to replace the SB, for in many ways this was less of a big leap forward than the SB had been 15 years earlier. By then, he says, 28,777 SBs had been built for the home and export markets and it seemed like a good time to call it a day. But the chassis refused to die. Spurred on mainly by export demand and sales

to the Ministry of Defence, it outlasted the model with which it was supposed to have been replaced and had practically doubled its 1965 sales total when it died with Bedford in 1986. The good Mr Townsin says the final tally was 57,129 – 'easily the highest total for any British bus or coach model'. Having clocked up 10,000 sales in 12 years, even the Dennis Dart has a long way to go to match that total.

Plaxton and Duple both built newer body designs on the SB, Duple gracing it with a version of its Dominant in the 1970s.

By then, we weren't supposed to call it the SB. Computerisation replaced letters and numbers with letters, which is why we were encouraged to think of this as the NJM. The N meant it was an SB, the J told us it had a 330cu in diesel and the M indicated a 7.3 to 8.6tonne gross vehicle weight. The petrol version by then would be an NFM. Strangely enough, the new designation just didn't stick. And are you surprised?

Although thought of mainly as a coach, the SB enjoyed some considerable success as a bus, mainly in rural areas and mainly with a Willowbrook or Duple (Midland) body. It was also popular with the military, with Mulliner and later Marshall bodywork, the latter having bought the former's bus bodying business and shipped it from Birmingham to Cambridge; readers of a certain age may recall the Mulliner-bodied SBs that provided airside services for a time at London Airport, as Heathrow was known at the dawn of the jet age.

There were a few other bigger players who used them. Walsall Corporation took six Willowbrook-bodied SBOs as early as 1956, at a time when the industry was experimenting with ever-lighter buses in a desperate attempt to cope with rapidly rising costs and rapidly declining patronage. About a dozen

One of the less common body makes on SB chassis was Thurgood of Ware, whose products were popular with East Anglian operators. New with Rose of Cheltenham, this example had passed to the fleet of Bunn of Walsingham when photographed in King's Lynn in 1958. The front panelling makes use of chrome fittings from contemporary Rootes Group models.
Michael Dryhurst

Left: *Although Bedford resisted calls for a front-entrance SB, coachbuilder Yeates produced this conversion, the Pegasus, and probably convinced Bedford that it could produce something similar, hence the later VAM model.*

Below left: *CIE built up a fleet of over 600 SB5s for school work throughout Ireland between 1968 and 1974. SS324 (PZO 324), seen here, is a 1969 example with bodywork built in Dundalk on Metal Sections frames and completed by CIE.*

years later, David MacBrayne started buying SB buses and coaches for its Scottish Highland and island services, having standardised on smaller Bedfords before then.

And then there was Bus Éireann. Or Coras Iompair Éireann, as it was then. Towards the end of the 1960s, Ireland – greatly influenced by the United States, to which so many of its population had emigrated – introduced universal free school transport with yellow school buses. Those buses were SBs and smaller VASs with utilitarian bodywork to a standard design built by a few commercial bodybuilders. They were joined in the mid-1970s by a few more with rather stylish Van Hool McArdle bodies – McArdle having built some of the older bodies before CIE coerced it into a short-lived joint venture with Van Hool.

As they wore out, most of the older models were replaced by ex-British MoD SB5s with Marshall bodies, later by all manner of exotic secondhand and cascaded vehicles, but the last Van Hool McArdles and ex-MoD Marshalls survived until 2001. Evidence enough, surely, that the SB is truly a wonderbus. **CB**

CROSVILLE MEMORABILIA

DAVID FLETCHER dips into his Crosville collection

The Million Mile Bus

Crosville made much of the fact that one of its Leyland Titans, TD2 no.M23, passed the million-mile mark. Passengers received an attractive souvenir booklet, and the local press covered the event – even if they got the registration wrong and described it as SM 6917, which might just have been a Caledonian bus.

Millionth Mile 1932 Crosville Bus Makes History

When a double-deck Crosville bus, SM6917, making its normal run on the Birkenhead to Chester route, reached Whitby roundabout just outside Ellesmere Port to-day, it completed its millionth mile since it was made in 1932.

To mark the occasion, the bus was pulled up and the passengers, mostly women shoppers, were asked to alight. They were given a souvenir booklet, and their fares were returned.

"GREAT TRIBUTE"

To the passengers on the roadside, Mr. J. R. Patey, assistant general manager of Crosville, said:—

"This is bus history. In some ways we are not proud of running a bus which has a million miles, but because of circumstances resulting from the war and the demand for exports we can no longer get the new vehicles at the rate we would like.

The fact that this bus has done a million miles is a great tribute to British engineering and to the men who have driven and maintained it."

The driver of the bus was 60-years-old Paul Newns, of Clare Avenue, Hoole, who took the first Crosville bus along the same route in 1911. With him as conductor was Sam Spilsbury, aged 68, who has been with the company 25 years.

The Crosville Company now owns 1,329 vehicles which cover 44,000,000 miles a year. There are 5,200 employees, and the company carries 170,000,000 passengers every year.

GOING FOR EXPORT

Answering criticisms which have reached the Echo about the age of buses on some routes in Wirral, Mr. F. P. Arnold, acting chairman of Crosville, said that owing to the export drive the number of buses available for home use had been considerably reduced.

Crosville's allocation for 1948 has not yet been fully delivered, and a number of buses have been allocated to the company have been diverted to London. Orders are already placed for 1949 and 1950 and the programme is being got out for 1951.

Dear Passenger,

The bus in which you are travelling has just completed its millionth mile since it was made in 1932. It is certainly no longer a new bus, being sixteen years old, but have a look at it and you will agree that we have tended it carefully during that time.

Every day of its long life it has moved over 172 miles of road, and there are very few vehicles in the country that have travelled so far in those many years—indeed, very few ever run a million miles at all. That distance is equivalent to going to the moon and back twice over !

Well, you—and other people like you—have made that feat possible, and this Company is not ungrateful for what you have done. We should, therefore, like you to be our guests on this particular trip on this bus (Reg. No. FM6917, Firm's No. M23), and to accept a present of the fare you have just paid for your ride, whether it is for a single or a return journey.

The Driver's name is___Paul Newns___and he has been__29__years in our service. Let us also introduce Conductor_____Sam Spilsbury._____who has now spent___25___years with us. They and our other 5,200 employees are doing their best for you and our other 170,000,000 passengers every year.

We shall certainly continue with our good work, not only because it is our living, but because we feel that we are pulling our weight in the affairs of the country.

Thank you once again for your support in the past, and we hope that we shall take you safely to your journey's end many times in the future.

25th January, 1949.

Yours faithfully,

CROSVILLE MOTOR SERVICES LTD.

As PART of its wartime public relations effort, Crosville commissioned a series of cartoons by *Punch* cartoonist Douglas England, which were incorporated into weekly press advertisements. Crosville's booklet about its wartime experiences, 'Crosville in Wartime', explained that 'It was hard to keep on telling the same old tale, but we did it'.

This is a selection of those adverts from the wartime and early postwar periods, displaying a rather forthright approach and a slightly black sense of humour!

INTERMEDIATE BUS STOPS

We get many complaints that buses run early from intermediate points.

Sometimes it is the clocks on the route.

Sometimes it is irregular loading.

Sometimes our staff can't get watches repaired.

THERE IS AN UNFAILING REMEDY

Be at the stop in good time, say five minutes before the bus is due. If you find it has gone, let us know as we shall want to make an investigation.

TAKING OUR MEDICINE

We have all had it pointed out to us that the nation's present suffering and inconvenience is caused by unwise government policy during the last twenty years.

That is so, and now we are taking our nasty medicine — it wouldn't do us much good if it wasn't nasty.

The medicine will cure us, so please think of this when travel is uncomfortable and there are delays, overcrowding, etc. It is all part of the medicine. We operators are getting our dose too in running the buses, but we stick it because we know that better times are coming.

WHY

We want you to leave peak hour buses for workpeople.

BECAUSE

These are the buses
That carry the folks
That go to the works
That make the shells
That fit the guns
That fire the shots
That wreck the planes
That carry the bombs
That may descend
And blitz the house
That YOU built.

Well, if that happens when you are at home you'll just HAVE to leave those peak hour buses for the right people, so why not

DO IT NOW?

WHY

We run last buses so early

BECAUSE

The petrol that we use so gaily
Comes across the ocean daily.
If we waste it running wildly
'Twould be a sin, to put it mildly.

> So get home early
> That's the style.
> Don't gad about
> It's not worth while.

BUT

When Blackpool's lights are
    shining brightly
We'll take you there and
    back twice nightly.

There is no room for Johnny Brown.

WHY

We try to allow long distance
passengers to take preference
over short distance people.

BECAUSE

If a bus has miles to run
And Billy Smith gets on,
There is no room for Johnny Brown
Who says he's travelling to a town
A hundred miles away.

But Billy Smith gets off again—
A penny fare just down the lane—
His seat is vacant—does he care?
Poor Johnny Brown (long distance fare)
Must walk it in the rain.

If Billy Smith would only walk
At times when seats are few,
Then Johnny Brown would find a place,
There'd be no waste of vacant space.
So now then, Billy, here's a case
Where Johnny gets your pew.

WHY

You must support your
employers if they suggest
staggering your hours.

BECAUSE

If all good people
Like you and me
Decide to go home
Together to tea
At half past five
Right on the dot,
It can't be done
Indeed it cannot
But half at six
And half at seven
We'll all get a ride
And that'll be heaven.

THE CONSULTATIVE COMMITTEE

A great deal is now being done to fit our available transport to your needs. All important areas are looked after by Consultative Committees.

In its simplest form each Committee consists of a bus man, a railway man, a working man (the poor passenger), a factory management man and a Civil Service man representing Government Departments.

These five know between them what is wanted. We have a certain limited number of buses and staff. The railway have a limited number of trains and crews. The Committee uses this equipment in the best possible way by saying who shall go by bus or train, and which factories shall have a call on these facilities at any particular time.

YOU CAN HELP

by supporting their recommendations. They are the only true solvers of the transport jig-saw in their area, as they know the needs and the amount of material available to fill those needs.

"THE LATE BILLY SMITH"

(ACCIDENTAL DEATH)

There was once a passenger named Billy Smith (a purely fictitious character). He did not mean any harm, but when he got on he rang the bell to start the bus. An old woman getting on after him was dragged along, fell, fractured her skull, and died.

He put his heavy bag on the rack, which was only meant for small parcels. As the bus went round a corner it fell off on to a girl's head and broke her neck.

When he got off, the bus had not stopped. Unfortunately he was facing the wrong way, and the road was harder than his head. He was dead when they got him to hospital.

Don't do any of these things. They are quite unnecessary and nearly always fatal. Even if a fool is born every day it need not be you.

'YOU CAN'T STOP IT THIS WAY'

ACCIDENTS

Dear Mr. Passenger,

Do you want to die in a stupid road accident before we have time to win the war? There is no need to do so if you will keep to the rules.

Our staff are attending special lectures and demonstrations on the subject of road accidents. The Police are helping by lending their traffic experts. But you must help, too.

The first lesson is getting on correctly.

(1) Wait till the bus stops.

(2) If it starts before you are on, let go quickly, even if you fall. If you hold on you will be dragged and will have to let go when the bus gets up speed. This means death or serious injury.

"LOOK AT THE RACK ABOVE YOUR HEAD"

ACCIDENTS

HOW TO AVOID TROUBLE WHEN ON THE BUS.

(1) Having got on correctly be sure to keep hold of one or more of the many handrails or straps while moving to your seat. If the bus starts or stops while you are on your feet you cannot then be thrown down. If it is moving you will have to hold on anyway.

(2) Before sitting down, look at the rack above your head. Maybe some bright soul has put a heavy bag up there which will fall and break your neck. Don't let anybody put one there as long as you occupy the seat.

(3) Don't ring the bell—you may cause a fatal accident.

"DON'T CROSS THE ROAD FROM BEHIND THE BUS"

ACCIDENTS

Having got on correctly and behaved correctly inside the bus, you will find yourself still alive, and therefore it is of the utmost importance to get off in the right way.

(1) Make sure the bus has stopped.

(2) Look each way to see that no vehicle can hit you, in case you are not at a kerb.

(3) Step off facing towards the front of the bus. If by any chance the bus is still moving, you will then not fracture your skull. Stepping off in any other direction will sooner or later involve you in a fatal accident.

(4) Be careful not to cross the road in front of the bus. Wait until it moves away. If you don't get killed this time you will the next.

THESE FOUR RULES GUARANTEE YOUR SAFETY.

No.1: Graham's Bus Service

CHECK POINT

Born: Linwood, Renfrewshire, 1929

Ended its days: 27 April 1990

What happened then?: J & W Graham began running a service between Johnstone and Glasgow with some single-deckers painted red. Along with other operators, Graham's belonged to the South Western Bus Owners' Association, one of several co-operatives set up by small operators to try and protect themselves against stiff competition which, in this case, came especially from Glasgow Corporation's high-frequency tram service. Even that was too much, and Graham's sold out to the newly-formed Western SMT in 1932.

But that wasn't the end of the story?: Not at all. Graham's recognised that it stood a better chance by applying for licences to provide links that its larger neighbours had yet to recognise. It ran from Linwood, which is to the west side of Paisley (then Scotland's largest town) to Hawkhead, to the south-eastern side of the town. It went on to move its base to Hawkhead, too. World War 2 brought an increase in business for Graham's, so its first double-deckers – ex-Glasgow Leyland Titan TD1s – were obtained. It got its first new utility Guy Arab in 1944.

The start of a transformation?: The start of several. More double-deckers followed, the company was reformed as Graham's Bus Service Ltd in May 1953 and around then the company's buses ceased to blush.

What?: Their livery changed from red and cream to orange and cream to maintain tradition and avoid confusion.

How or why did it do that?: Orange and cream (with a maroon band) had been the colours of Paisley's major operator, Young's and Paisley & District, until it was taken over by Western in 1950/1. Western, until then, was a comparatively insignificant operator in the area, so the similarity between its colours and those of Graham's wasn't an issue. But the steady repainting of ex-Young's and P&D buses into red threatened to swamp Graham's which spotted the obvious solution. Adopt orange for itself.

And the company grew again?: It started another service between Elderslie, to the west of Linwood, and Penilee, a wartime housing estate on Glasgow's western edges, in 1958 and extended it a year later into Govan Cross, then one of the centres of Clyde shipbuilding and one of the busiest stations on Glasgow's underground railway. It also benefited from one of the bigger blunders of British car manufacturing.

Which was?: The Hillman Imp. The Rootes Group wanted to build its rear-engined compact car at Dunstable, but the government of the day favoured supporting areas whose traditional industries (like shipbuilding) were in decline. Rootes was sent to Scotland and picked a site at Linwood, where Pressed Steel had already set up shop building car bodies and trains. As the road service licence holder for the road into Linwood, Graham's was in a privileged position. Its fleet, carryings and service network grew, especially after Imp production began in 1962, by which time it was moving on to rear-engined double-deckers in the shape of Fleetlines mainly, Atlanteans mainly in later years. And Linwood would play another part in Graham's expansion.

When was that?: In 1977 Greater Glasgow PTE decided against building a railway station there and instead persuaded Graham's and Western SMT to provide a motorway express service into Glasgow. It was called the Linwood Clipper and it was an overnight success. This was perhaps the company's finest hour.

What went wrong?: General decline was hitting Graham's as much as everyone else, but the fiasco of the Imp was followed by problems with other cars produced there, and Peugeot (which by then owned the former Rootes business) closed the plant around 1980. Then along came deregulation and the company lost all heart.

Who took over?: Its end wasn't as simple as that. The family put the company up for sale in 1990, but it seems no one put in an offer they wanted to accept. Instead, Strathclyde Buses bought four Volvo B10Ms, registered replacement services and took on most of the staff. But the company just fizzled to a stop in the middle of the last afternoon. A sad end for a much-loved company.

Alan Millar

Graham's first Daimler Fleetline, and one of the first in Scotland – no.60 (GXS 621) of 1963 with Alexander body, seen on an Omnibus Society Scottish Branch tour when it was new, with your editor, considerably younger and slimmer, on the front platform.
Robert Grieves

PRESELECTOR
ARAB IIIs

**DAVID HARVEY on the postwar Guy double-deckers
that featured this gearbox**

*The largest single batch of double-deck preselector Arab IIIs were
45 for Belfast Corporation. These buses were bodied by Harkness
which for the first time used Metal Sections frames rather than the
previously used Park Royal frames. The result was a most
attractive-looking five-bay construction body which is seen here in
almost original condition, only the legend BELFAST CORPORATION
being omitted from the lower-saloon waistrail. No.334 is working
on the 90 route to Donegall Road. The bus is in Donegall Square
East, behind Belfast's City Hall.*
R Marshall

O F ALL the British psv chassis manufacturers,
Wolverhampton-based Guy Motors could
justifiably claim that 'it had A Good War',
between 1939 and 1945. At the beginning of the
conflict the Wolverhampton-based company had
been a comparatively small-sized manufacturer of
light to medium weight vans and lorries. As far as
the psv market was concerned, the lorry-derived
Wolf 2-tonner, and Vixen 3-4-tonner, were bodied in
small numbers as 20-odd seater buses and coaches.
Production of the larger Arab model, first offered in

An early Wolverhampton Brush-bodied Guy Arab III, no.398, stands in Princes Street near the junction with Queen Street, Wolverhampton, very early in its career. It is working on the 15 route to Codsall. This style of body was also found on two small batches of Arab IIIs for Gateshead & District and Northern General, but there the similarity ends as the Wolverhampton buses all had the larger Gardner 6LW engine and the preselector gearbox option. The option for these first postwar Wolverhampton buses was the sliding cab door, while the unusual bright green and bright yellow livery with two black bands suited these buses very well.
W J Haynes

The third batch of preselector gearbox Arab IIIs were the 7-16 group of Guy-bodied vehicles for Newport Corporation. They were fitted with the 10.35-litre Meadows 6DC engine, which because of its compact nature enabled the radiator to be fitted flush with the cab front apron. No.16 is working on the 30 route from Newport to Cardiff in its first few years of service, as after July 1954 the powerful but awkward-to-work-on Meadows engines were gradually removed from each of these ten buses, a process which was completed by January 1956.
R H G Simpson

1933 as the first double-decker exclusively listed with only an oil-engine, had virtually ground to a halt with only Burton-upon-Trent Corporation ordering the model, albeit in single-decker form, after 1937.

By late 1945, when Daimler and Bristol were starting their postwar PSV chassis production based on their wartime products and AEC, Crossley and Leyland were introducing their new models, there was a Midlands-based competitor who was already well established with an existing chassis. A new design of Guy Arab double-decker had been allocated to bus operators by the Ministry of War Transport and was initially welcomed very reluctantly as being better than having nothing at all. The bus was fitted with a sliding-mesh crash gearbox and was generally only made available with the Gardner 5LW, 7.0-litre engine, making it underpowered, sluggish and hard work to drive. Yet the robust construction of the chassis, based around drawings of the stillborn Leyland Titan TD8, quickly drew a large following. Municipal operators and BET companies became willing recipients and purchasers of the new Arab, and after the first 500 the more common Arab II version quickly gained a reputation for being a robust, well-made bus. When operators began to place their first postwar orders, Guy Motors was well placed to exploit its existing chassis.

The cessation of hostilities meant that lighter

The nearside front view of London Transport G436 at Chingford station, in about 1952, when working on the 121 service, shows just how little the Guy body differed from the standard layout of this model when delivered to 'provincial' operators. Although the bus had a Guy body to Park Royal design, this standard and, it has to be said, successful metal-framed body did not compare too favourably when parked alongside a Park Royal body of similar vintage mounted on an RT chassis.
A M Wright

aluminium alloys became available once again. The use of this material enabled the weight of the MkII chassis to be significantly reduced, and with other modifications this became the new Arab III model. The cranking of the horizontal radiator mounting bar over the engine enabled a 4in reduction in the bonnet line, though the frontal aspect of the wartime Arab II was in part retained, as the 'curly' front wings were retained on the new model. The whole frontal design was further enhanced by the adoption of a polished aluminium radiator surmounted with the Indian Chief's head and the Guy legend 'Feathers in their Cap'.

Initially the new Arab III model was introduced as 17ft 6in wheelbase single-decker in March 1946, but it was not until early 1947 that the double-decker version with a 16ft 3in wheelbase was introduced. Both models were available with the existing Gardner 7.0-litre, 5LW or 8.4-litre, 6LW engine inherited from the previous Arab II chassis. In some ways this was rather ironic as throughout the war period the larger Gardner 6LW engine was a comparatively rare beast, being ostensibly allocated by the Ministry of War Transport to operators of the Arab and Arab II model which worked in hilly areas. The Arab III was also available with the huge 10.35-litre Meadows 6DC engine. This splendidly powerful yet economical and compact unit was available after the autumn of 1948. Unfortunately, its power belied an unacceptable level of repair on an engine which was difficult to work on, and as a result of this the option for the Wolverhampton-built engine was dropped on the Arab III model in 1951.

Normally, the brakes offered on the Arab III were triple-servo vacuum, although Westinghouse air

brakes were an optional extra. The new chassis was offered with a single-plate clutch and a four-speed constant-mesh gearbox. This was a distinct improvement over the wartime 'crash' unit, which had straight-toothed gears and initially a reversed 'H' layout to the gearbox, with 1st and 2nd gears on the right. Chassis numbers of the double-decker Arab III appear to have begun with FD35904 and reached FD36279 on right hand-drive chassis and FD38603 on left-hand drive chassis, before, in 1949, a new series was begun at FD70000.

Success

Sales of the Guy Arab III were a great success, capitalising on the reputation gained during the war for robust construction coupled with the economic operating costs of the Gardner engines. The competition in a postwar market desperate for new buses was very keen and although Leyland Motors did not manufacture an 'easy-change' gearbox for either its Titan PD1 or PD2 double-decker, AEC, with its Regent III, and Daimler, with its CVA, CVD and CVG models, both offered a preselector gearbox option, which in the case of Daimler meant a Wilson fluid flywheel. This left Guy Motors at a distinct disadvantage and development work was put in place to redress this situation. In 1948, a four-speed Wilson fluid-flywheel, preselector epicyclic gearbox option was made available. So it would not infringe the Daimler steering column-mounted gearchange patents, the preselector Arab III model had the gearchange lever placed on the floor in the position of the normal gear lever to the left of the driver and was given a smaller knob top distinguish it from the more normal constant-mesh gear lever. In addition,

the fluid-flywheel and the preselector gearbox were remotely mounted 'amidships' away from the engine.

The resultant preselector Arab III was, however, something of a rare beast. In single-deck form, fewer than 50 were built, with 25 of these going to Belfast Corporation and Wolverhampton having ten. The other municipalities to have them were Accrington and Sunderland. The double-deck production again was disappointing. While the BET Group, particularly East Kent, Northern General and Gateshead & District, 'enjoyed' the rigours of the manual-gearbox Arab III, the municipalities generally fought shy of the new preselector gearbox Arab III. This was a great pity, as here was a bus that could compete directly with the Daimler CVG6 for the 'easy-change' market. This was at a time when many municipal operators were getting rid of their trams and were looking for an option which would be 'driver-friendly' and have a gearbox that would be easy to master.

Guy's hometown of Wolverhampton was the first recipient of the Arab III in its preselector gearbox form, which carried on the tradition begun in 1934 when two preselector Daimler COG5 single-deckers were purchased. In 1936 it bought a solitary Arab which had a Brush body. This Gardner 5LW-powered vehicle was fitted with a four-speed Wilson epicyclic gearbox, although Guy Motors briefly in the mid-1930s offered a less successful French-designed Cotal electro-magnetically-controlled epicyclic gearbox. Wolverhampton Corporation turned to the Daimler COG5 to its normal specification of a Wilson fluid flywheel and preselector gearbox for nearly all its prewar needs. Having received 24 wartime Arab and Arab II models, Wolverhampton ordered 40 preselector Arab IIIs once they became available. Dual-

sourcing its first postwar orders with Brush-bodied Daimler CVG6 chassis, 18 of the Arab IIIs had composite H29/25R Brush bodies. These came as 384-98 (FJW 384-98) and 536-8 (FJW 536-8), with the first six, 384-9, entering service in 1948. The remaining 22, nos.539-60, (FJW 539-60), had Park Royal H28/26R bodies and were delivered in 1950. Although some were withdrawn as early as 1963, a few soldiered-on into the ownership of West Midlands PTE. The preselector gearbox specification of this first postwar Wolverhampton order initiated a trend for the rest of the lifetime of the Corporation, as after this order for Arab IIIs the Corporation Transport Committee specified the later Arab IV and V models, which well-built chassis with the preselector gearbox option coupled to cheap bodywork.

The contemporary ten Arab III single-deckers, 561-5 (FJW 561-5) with Guy B34R bodywork and 566-70 (FJW 566-70) with Park Royal B34R bodies to a design unique to UK operators, had Gardner 5LW engines. Unlike their double-deck counterparts these ten were all withdrawn by 1963.

The second municipality to buy the new preselector gearbox option was Newport Corporation. In late 1948 and early 1949 this undertaking received nos.7-16 (FDW 41-50), which were ten Meadows-engined Arab IIIs. The first one, was exhibited at the 1948 Commercial Motor Show and had fluorescent interior saloon lights. The double-deckers were a sufficient success to warrant a repeat order for another ten of these Guy-bodied buses with Park Royal framework. These came at the end of 1949 and early 1950 as nos.17-26 (FDW 841-50) but had the less powerful,but more robust Gardner 6LW engines.

G436

After supplying London Transport with 71 of the first wartime Arab model (later to be called the Mark I) and 364 Arab IIs between December 1942 and April 1946, orders for Guys from the Capital dried up. As a speculative venture, in the hope to gain an order, a single vehicle was supplied by Guy in January 1950. The bus was the short-lived G436 (KGK 981). This Arab III with its 'easy-change' pre-selector gearbox and Wilson fluid flywheel was an attempt by the Fallings Park-based company to break the stranglehold of orders for the AEC Regent O961RT and the Leyland Titan 7RT in London, although it is a moot point as to whether the vehicle was ever indeed ordered by LT as the evidence suggests that G436 was given to it by Guy Motors.

As a one-off vehicle in the world's most standardised bus fleet, poor old KGK never stood a chance! It was immediately at a disadvantage as it was fitted with the powerful but expensive-to-maintain Meadows 6DC engine. G436 had a Guy H30/26R body built on Park Royal steel frames and was the first of all the preselector Arab IIIs to be withdrawn by its original owner. Although it had London Transport destination boxes, offside stencil route holder and running number holders on each side underneath the front lower saloon windows, G436 always looked what in reality it was – a provincial bus masquerading as a vehicle suitable for the conditions in London. It was, with the obvious exception of the gearbox, virtually the same as the splendid 3557-76 (MHA 57-76) of Midland Red and with not a too dissimilar livery might have been better off finishing off its days pounding up and down the hills of the Black Country based in Dudley.

As it turned out, G436 ran from Old Kent Road garage for just over 17 months before moving on for a short stay at Nunhead garage. From 1952 until its premature withdrawal in February 1955, G436 worked from Enfield garage, before being bought for export in July 1955 to Yugoslavia where, somewhat ironically, it lasted longer than in London.

The largest order for Arab IIIs with preselector gearboxes came from that often forgotten UK municipality, Belfast Corporation. Its bus fleet had expanded considerably during World War 2, with the wartime growth of the Harland & Wolff shipyard and Short Brothers aircraft factory on the shores of Belfast Lough. Although 43 wartime Daimler CWA6s were bought new, along with seven unpopular Arab IIs with quite awful Pickering 'utility' bodies, the Corporation fleet was further augmented with 29 Bedford OWBs and 20 secondhand prewar Leyland Tigers and AEC Regals, mostly fitted with totally unsuitable coach bodywork.

The need for new buses was beginning to become a real problem; the Belfast tram system was in terminal decline and although the splendid trolleybus fleet was still expanding, the 40 early Daimler CVA6s were no where near enough to meet the growing traffic demands. Having already ordered 70 six-wheel Guy BTX trolleybuses, the general manager, Col R McCreary, impressed with the build quality of the Arab II chassis, if not with the buses themselves, became aware that Guy Motors could give an early delivery date for a batch of 45 double and 25 single-deck Arab IIIs. They were all fitted with Wilson fluid flywheels and preselector gearbox and all had Gardner 6LW 8.4-litre engines. Both the double-deckers, 305-49 (MZ 7403-47), and the single-

Seen at the Fallings Park works of Guy Motors in the spring of 1949, this was a late mock-up front design for the Arab III Specials with the 'new-look' front for Birmingham City Transport. The bonnet and front assembly are very close to the finished article, but the nearside front wing, with its thick profile and the wing-mounted side lights, would be altered on the finished product. The offside front wing is just visible and this is still of the exposed radiator upturned style usually associated with the Arab III model.
D R H collection

deckers, 280-304 (MZ 7378-402), had bodies built by Harkness Coach Works of McTier Street, Belfast, but for the first time all were completed on Metal Sections frames, built in Oldbury in the West Midlands. Within two years of entering service, all the Guys had to have their original flexibly-mounted bodies, which were specified by the Corporation, rebuilt at Belfast's expense with rigid body fixings, due to the excessive bodyroll and play in the mountings. All the single-deck Arab IIIs were delivered in 1950, but only 305-38 of the double-deckers arrived that year, the balance of the order, 339-49, arriving in the first few months of 1951, indeed being the only vehicles delivered to Belfast in the course of that year.

The good-looking single-deckers, with only a seating capacity of 31, did not fare too well as regards longevity; the first ones went as early as 1958, although six did last until 1970. On the other hand, the double-deckers were particularly long-lived, with some surviving beyond the 2 April 1973 take-over of Belfast Corporation by Citybus, including the lovingly restored no.346. The double-deckers, although looking a little squashed at 26ft long, were splendid vehicles, seemingly being a lot more powerful than the slightly newer Daimler CVG6s, although this was due mainly to the rasping exhaust fitted to the Guys, rather than the more refined and muffled noise emanating from a CVG6.

Order

Another small municipal order for the preselector Arab III came from South Shields Corporation, which ordered two double-deckers. This pair was delivered in May and June 1950 in reverse numerical order. They were numbered 146/7 (CU 5226/7) and were fitted with Gardner 6LW engines and, unusually, bodies built by Barnard. These attractive-looking

H30/26R bodies from the Norwich-based coachbuilder, along with a lone Daimler CVD6 from the previous year, were the only Barnard double-deck bodies supplied in the north-east. Nos.146/7 also appear to have been the only Guy Arabs bodied by Barnard, with Daimler CVD6s and AEC Regent IIIs more typically being the recipients of this manufacturer's bodywork. Nos.146/7 lasted slightly longer than most Barnard composite bodies, which had a tendency to become a little frail without major rebuilding, with 147 going in 1964 and its twin in the following year.

The penultimate batch of 'pure' Arab IIIs with preselector gearboxes and fluid flywheels were supplied between October and December 1952. These vehicles were delivered to Sunderland Corporation and were numbered 128-38 (CBR 528-38). There was a twelfth bus in the batch, numbered 139 (CBR 539), which was built with a constant-mesh gearbox. Two years earlier, Sunderland had received two of the even rarer pre-selector Arab III single-deckers which had Roe B35F bodies. All 12 double-deckers had Gardner 6LW engines and Charles Roe H33/25R bodies which were constructed to the attractive 'Pullman' design which had been introduced by Roe only about a year earlier. Costing exactly £4,000 each, they weighed in an exactly 8 tons, and coincidentally, the 'preselector 11' were the only 8ft-wide ones to be built. The eleven lasted until 1966, but ironically the constant-mesh

The completed bus. Birmingham City Transport no.2530, photographed in July 1950 by Metro-Cammell prior to delivery to Quinton garage, shows off its 'new-look' front as well as the wheel discs which somehow seemed to finish off the classical lines of a tin-fronted Birmingham bus. So was it an Arab III, an Arab III Special, a Birmingham Arab or an Arab IV? Whatever it was, it was an extremely well-finished and handsome-looking bus, whose sound construction enabled this particular bus to have a working life of 24 years – and remember, there were no postwar body swaps in Birmingham!
MCCW

vehicle, now renumbered 242, survived in service until 1972, partly in a role as a driver trainer, and was sold for preservation.

The final Arab III double-deckers to be built for any operator were also the last ten supplied to Southampton Corporation and were delivered to the undertaking between December 1953 and September 1954. These last Arab IIIs were numbered 64-73 (LOW 210-9) and in common with the rest of the Southampton vehicles had the by now rather conservative seating capacity of H30/26R. Southampton had received a total of 150 Park Royal-bodied examples between March 1948 and 1954 and by the time they were delivered the buses looked distinctly old-fashioned. This conservative ordering policy did have the advantage of standardising the fleet on a well-tried and quite robust body coupled to the faithful Gardner 6LW engine. The body was of the same design as those nominally built by Guy itself on Park Royal frames for the aforementioned 'London One' and the 20 supplied to Newport Corporation. What made nos.64-73 different was that they had Wilson fluid-flywheels and pre-elector gearboxes, which must have come as a shock to the double-declutch bus driving fraternity of Southampton. Most of the batch were taken out of service in 1971, but happily no.71 (LOW 217) was retained by the Corporation for preservation.

Contradictory

Yet there was one more, large batch of Wilson fluid flywheel, preselector epicyclic gearbox Arabs, but there are contradictory explanations as to what they were! In late 1948, Birmingham City Transport decided that a new style of front end would enhance the look of the smartly presented fleet as well as

competing with Midland Red which was beginning to introduce new double-deckers with its own style of concealed radiator. Birmingham had been an 'easy-change' fleet since 1934 and had mainly used Daimlers for its bus requirements, although a policy of dual-sourcing in the latter part of the 1930s led to the development of the Leyland Titan TD6c, specifically for BCT, with the smooth, but hardly fuel-efficient Lysholm-Smith torque converter transmission system. After the end of World War 2, Birmingham's main orders again went to Daimler and initially, Leyland Motors with its Titan PD2/1, 201 entering service, including the second of only two PD2s ever built, HOJ 396, (see the book *The Forgotten Double Deckers* Part One, Chapter One 'The Grand Daddy Of Them All'). Contractual problems with Leyland, coupled to its unwillingness at that stage to get involved with an preselector option. led to BCT looking elsewhere for its requirements. Having placed an order with Crossley Motors of Stockport for 270 DD42/6s with synchromesh gearboxes, only to discover that Crossley would be taking no new orders after 1950, following its take-over by ACV, Birmingham had to again look elsewhere for a manufacturer of new buses which were becoming desperately needed with the imminent closure of the tram and trolleybus systems in the city.

Birmingham turned to Guy Motors, which had not long before announced its new preselector option on the Arab III, and placed an order for 100 double-deckers. Just as had been the case with Crossleys, what Birmingham specified for its initial order of 26ft-long Arabs was distinctly more than was the standard vehicle manufactured at Fallings Park. To meet the requirements of BCT, Guy's design staff

produced a new basic chassis frame without a platform extension and with a 16ft 4in wheelbase, new flexible engine mountings and a Gardner 6LW engine coupled to a fluid flywheel and 4-speed epicyclic preselector gearbox which was mounted amidships in the chassis. At the same time as the chassis redesign work was taking place, in the spring of 1949 BCT and Guy developed a series of mock-up fronts, including a strange-looking full-fronted version. A sheet-metal front was also fitted to no.1852 (HOV 852), a 1949 Daimler CVG6 which entered service, after its experimental start to life, on 15 December 1948.

Hijacked

Then the whole project was somewhat hijacked by Crossley, which sensationally, on 27 February 1950, enabled Birmingham to place in service no.2426, (JOJ 426). This was the first of 100 Crossleys fitted with concealed radiators, whose long front cowling vaguely looked like Christian Dior's New Look skirt length. (Just as an aside, it has always bothered me – did Christian Dior ever know he was a bus front designer?) The 'new-look' bus front was born and Guy, which had been at the forefront of the development work, had been upstaged by a company which was going out of business, yet got all the publicity! The Crossley 'new-look' front was a bit of a cheat as it was a sheet metal cowl, bonnet and wings covering the existing exposed radiator front. This is why Crossley was able to steal such a march over its competitors. Have a look under the bonnet of the author's well-known no.2489 (JOJ 489) and the ruse

is instantly revealed! The 2526-2625 batch had their front ends built up from scratch as a completely new assembly which was designed in such a way that any bodybuilder would have little problem in integrating into its own coachwork.

The first of the short-length, heavyweight Guys, no.2526 (JOJ 526) entered service on 4 July 1950, by which time 55 of the last 'new look front' Crossleys had entered service. The last of these MCCW H30/24R-bodied Arab buses, which weighed 8tons 2cwt, no.2625 (JOJ 625) entered service on 4 May 1951 and some of the late survivors were destined to be among the last Birmingham halfcabs to remain in service, only being withdrawn on 31 October 1977 when West Midlands PTE finally converted the famous 11 Outer Circle route to rear-engined Daimler Fleetlines. From this class of 100, no fewer than four are preserved. As a result of this successful order another 201 Guy Arabs were ordered, the last coming in October 1954.

What were these first 100 Birmingham Guys? Guy certainly referred to the first 100 as 'Birmingham Arabs', but the Corporation had them down as 'Arab III Specials'! Nos.2526-2625 were in reality a halfway house between the MkIII and the MkIV. They were based on the Arab III and as such deserve a full account of their origins in this article as they were obviously fitted with preselector epicyclic gearboxes.

But then what about the other 201 Arabs which were built to a length of 27ft? The classification for these is Arab IV, though they too were known at Guy Motors as 'Birmingham Arabs' because the chassis

did not have the normal Arab IV drop-frame platform extension. These longer buses were numbered 2901-94 (JOJ 901-94) and 3003-102, (MOF 3-102), all of which had MCCW H30/25R bodies which weighed a fraction over 8tons. In addition this batch included nos.2995-3000 (JOJ 995-9 and LOG 300), which looked the same but sounded totally different as they had David Brown constant-mesh gearboxes. The missing one was no.3001 (LOG 301). This had a Birmingham-lookalike lightweight Saunders-Roe H30/25R body which was fitted to a chassis which was originally going to be Guy's equivalent of the Daimler CLG5. In the event FD71257 was turned out by Guy as a virtually standard chassis but with lightweight chassis components with the complete bus weighing 7tons 5cwt. All 201 of these Birmingham Arab IVs were fitted with Gardner 6LW engines, but no.3001 was re-engined with a prewar rebuilt Gardner 5LW unit from a Daimler COG5 as early as June 1953.

Arab IV

From the initial batch of 100 buses for Birmingham was born the Arab IV, although the new model, unlike the Birmingham vehicles, had a drop-frame extension and a 4-speed constant-mesh gearbox as

standard. From 1951 until 1953 the Arab IV was only offered with the Birmingham-style 'new look front' but in Coronation year an exposed radiator option was introduced. The first production Arab IVs were ten Weymann-bodied examples for Lancashire United which entered service in 1951 as nos.452-61 (MTJ 91-100). Thus for about three years Arab III production ran alongside the new Arab IV model.

Between the announcement in 1948 of the preselector gearbox option on the Arab III and the cessation of production in 1954, only 148 double-deckers with this option were produced. This must have been a considerable disappointment to the Guy Motors staff at Fallings Park, Wolverhampton, who must have felt that the Wilson fluid flywheel and

The last ten of the Arab IIIs to be supplied to Southampton Corporation were fitted with preselector gearboxes. They were also the last Arab IIIs to be built, though their Park Royal metal-framed bodies could have been constructed to this design some eight years earlier. A somewhat grimy-looking no.67, fitted with the Cave-Browne-Cave heating and ventilator system, waits at Woolstone when working on the circular service in company with a later East Lancs-bodied AEC Regent V.
D R H collection

preselector gearbox option coupled to the robust Arab III chassis and Gardner 6LW engine (although not perhaps the alternative Meadows 6DC option) was a potential challenger to Daimler as the third place manufacturer of double-deckers in the UK. Within the statistics of the preselector Arab III production, all bar the ten for Sunderland were 7ft 6in wide and 147 of the 148 went to municipalities. Guy had been quite keen to get into the BET Group orders but no orders for the option were placed. It was only well into the Arab IV era that the traditional 'stick-change' began to give way to something a little easier.

The Guy Arab III in its preselector gearbox form always seemed to be something of an afterthought and it was only when Birmingham became interested that this alternative form of transmission began to become something more than a minority option, although by then the Arab III was on its way out and would be completely replaced by the Arab IV chassis. **CB**

THE PRESELECTOR GUY ARAB IIIs

Wolverhampton Corporation
384-98 (FJW 384-98) 6LW. Brush H29/25R, 1949
536-8 (FJW 536-8) 6LW. Brush H29/25R, 1949
539-60 (FJW 539-60) 6LW. Park Royal H28/26R, 1950

Newport Corporation
7-16 (FDW 41-50) 6DC. Guy H30/26R, 1949
17-26 (FDW 841-50) 6LW. Guy H30/26R, 1949 (17-21)
1950 (22-6)

London Transport
G436 (KGK 981) 6DC. Guy H30/26R, 1/50

Belfast Corporation
305-49 (MZ 7403-47) 6LW. Harkness H28/26R, 1950

Birmingham City Transport
2526-625 (JOJ 526-625) 6LW. MCCW H30/24R, 7/50-5/51

South Shields Corporation
146/7 (CU 5226/7) 6LW. Barnard H30/26R, 5-6/52

Sunderland Corporation
128-38 (CBR 528-38) 6LW. Roe H33/25R, 10 & 12/52

Southampton Corporation
64-73 (LOW 210-9) 6LW. Park Royal H30/26R, 12/53-9/54

A SAFE BET

The British Electric Traction group (BET) successfully ran a significant proportion of the company buses in England and Wales for many years, staying out of state-ownership until 1968 when its acquisition by the Transport Holding Company was a prelude to the formation of the National Bus Company. Unlike its state-owned sister, Tilling, BET encouraged its companies to continue in their existing liveries. These TED JONES photos remember BET vehicles in all their glory

Above: *Ribble's fleet became almost as distinctive as Southdown's for its 30ft long full-fronted designs of the 1957-63 period, although the livery was much less attractive. However, they had been preceded by 120 Leyland Titan halfcabs in 1955-6, here exemplified by Metro-Cammell Orion-bodied PD2/13 no.1400, with enclosed rear platform, approaching Prescot on service 320 from Wigan to Liverpool in July 1968, then operated jointly with Lancashire United and the corporations of Wigan and St Helens; one of the latter's Orion-bodied PD2 passes by.*
All photos by Ted Jones

Below: *An animated scene in Stockport's Mersey Square in May 1971, arguably the major hub of North Western Road Car's widespread stage carriage operations, as well as those of the municipality, by then absorbed within the Selnec PTE. No.120 was a 1964 AEC Renown 3B3RA with Park Royal 72-seat body, which would itself become a Selnec bus later in 1971 for a final four years' service. On the left are two ex-corporation buses, the saloon already having been repainted into PTE colours.*

Above: *Not at all what it seems! This innocuous-looking Plaxton-bodied coach in Shrewsbury's Barker Street bus station in October 1969 was in fact one of Midland Red's 'in-house' C3 models built in 1954 as no.4239 and rebodied eight years later, enabling it to serve the company for a further nine years or so. In 1963 it had re-entered service in an all-cream livery, but in response to local sentiment had been repainted in red with a black roof the following year, and finally, in 1967, to the red and maroon layout portrayed here.*

Left: *Parked outside PMT's headquarters in Stoke-on-Trent after repainting for preservation, to represent the most florid exception to PMT's usually uninspired red-based liveries, this export-model Leyland Titan OPD2/1 had an interesting history. It had entered service in 1949 as Weymann-bodied single-decker no.453, receiving this 1951-built NCME lowbridge body with standee lower-deck windows from a prewar Titan TD4 in 1954, to become no.L453, until sold to an East Anglian operator nine years later.*

Above: *Yorkshire Woollen District was another fleet in which a sombre livery (maroon and cream) was superseded in 1953 by an equally dreary one (unrelieved red) only slightly improved on deckers by the addition of a cream band in the 1960s. This final stage is represented by Roe-bodied Leyland PD2A/30 no.135 of 1958, acquired in January 1970 when Sheffield's 'C' fleet was disbanded. Renumbered 466 just three months after this August 1971 view in Dewsbury, it was to serve YWD for barely three years.*

Below: *Trent Motor Traction was an early customer for Leyland's revolutionary Atlantean, and this PDR1/1 model of 1962, with Weymann 77-seat bodywork, was amongst the third batch to be acquired. Garbed in the simplified later-postwar livery, no.465 is leaving Alfreton on limited-stop service X1 to Derby, in September 1968.*

Above: *The unique traditional East Yorkshire Motor Services livery of indigo, primrose and white had seemingly disappeared for ever after the NBC takeover, only to be successfully revived for the Routemasters acquired for Hull city services in 1988/9. No. 806, formerly London Transport RM1271, seemed in fine fettle for a 26-year old when sweeping round Queen's Gardens in the city centre in August 1988.*

Below: *Unlike some sister companies, Yorkshire Traction maintained the same livery styling for its double-deckers throughout the postwar BET era, well portrayed here by Leyland Titan PD3A/1 no.746 with Roe bodywork, arriving in the centre of Wakefield in May 1971. The Huddersfield rather than Barnsley registration of this 1964-built 73-seater betrays it to be one of the acquisitions from the January 1971 break-up of jointly-owned County Motors of Lepton, and it would serve its new fleet for only five years.*

Above: *A sharp comparison between Tilling and BET coaching policy is afforded by this Victoria Coach Station cameo from April 1968. On the left is Thames Valley's no.D8, a 1964 ECW-bodied Bristol Lodekka FLF6G with coach seating, signified by the South Midland-derived livery, on one of the frequent express services from London to Reading. On the right is a 36ft long 1963 AEC Reliance 2U3RA with Park Royal dual-purpose bodywork, 6544 FN, from the Canterbury-based East Kent fleet, offering a coach-air connection to Paris, via Lympne (Kent) and Beauvais airports. Some 1962 deliveries of this type were painted in a pale blue Skybus-dedicated livery for the service.*

Below: *For barely a year from 1971, NBC's amalgamation of BET's Southdown and Tilling's Brighton, Hove, & District fleets caused typical Tilling vehicle types to appear in the former company's livery. Here is 1962-built Bristol Lodekka FSF6B no.2037 with 60-seat ECW forward-entrance bodywork, awaiting a crew change outside Whitehawk garage in September 1973, transmuted from red and cream, and destined to give just over two more years' service.*

Above: *Aldershot & District Traction had a surprisingly long affinity with Dennis chassis, even allowing for the latter's factory being 'on the patch'. Built during one of Dennis's 'stop-go' phases of psv production, when Loline chassis were intermittently offered as non-embargoed versions of Bristol's highly-successful Lodekkas, no.357 was a 1958 delivery with shapely East Lancs 68-seat bodywork, complete with doors to its rear platform. It was the only Mk1 version to see brief service with the successor Alder Valley company in 1972, and is seen here soon after restoration to its original condition.*

Below: *Caught in Sea Road, Bexhill, in November 1969, just two years before withdrawal, no.3216 was one of Maidstone & District's first batch of AEC Reliance buses. An MU3RV model with Weymann 41-seat bodywork that had entered service early in 1957, it well portrays the company's distinctive traditional livery so soon to be dropped in favour of NBC's undistinguished leaf-green and white.*

Above: BET's 1951 takeover of Thomas Bros (Port Talbot) as an amalgam of small operators had some resonance with the Tilling Group's formation of Durham District Services, but with typically greater autonomy it was an ideal training ground for budding managers. By the mid 1960s regular BET specifications had displaced the rich variety of inherited vehicles, and this July 1965 view shows AEC Reliance 124 SNY of 1963 with Marshall 53-seat body and offside illuminated advertisement panel. In pursuit is a 1954 Saunders-Roe-bodied Tiger Cub, both buses wearing the steel-blue livery unique to this operator.

Below: Heading down the A49 near Craven Arms on a Blackpool-Shrewsbury-Cheltenham express service in April 1972, with the Long Mynd as a backdrop, Black & White Motorways' no.229 was a 36ft long Plaxton Panorama-bodied Leyland Leopard PSU3/3R. It still presented a good image, although by then 10 years old, but when new, black upperworks had made the livery even more distinctive. The company was two-thirds owned by BET and one-third by the Tilling Group, with its operating base at Cheltenham coach station, but registered office at BMMO's Bearwood, Birmingham, HQ.

Above: *Sporting Grey Cars of Torquay's traditional livery, which looked much better than National Express all-over white on this 1979 Duple-bodied Leyland Leopard PSU5C, no.193 heads away from Torquay Harbour with just a few passengers on a local excursion in May 1987. Grey Cars had been a Devon General subsidiary from 1932 until NBC days, when both came under Western National control, but the fleetname and goodwill were obviously valuable enough to justify exception to NBC's strict policy on suppression of local identities, perhaps to counter local competition for day-tours.*

Left: *Amongst the last buses to receive City of Oxford's unique traditional livery were the Northern Counties-bodied lowheight dual-door Fleetlines delivered in 1969, represented here by no.396 in June 1972. Lacking the design flair of Park Royal's similar contemporary design, this was arguably one of the less-attractive products of the Wigan company, and looks almost ramshackle in this view on Magdalen Bridge.*

1982

It was 20 years ago, just at the point when CB recognises a Classic Bus. GAVIN BOOTH looks back at what was old and what was new that year

Left: *Some things never change. A scene you could almost recreate today – London Transport Routemaster RML2652 rounds Parliament Square in April 1982. Note the advertising for Adam and the Ants' 'Prince Charming'.*
All photos by Gavin Booth

Above: *Stranger on LT's Round London Sightseeing Tour in Whitehall in April, London Country AN116, a Metro-Cammell-bodied Leyland Atlantean PDR1A/1 Special, one of four hired, with drivers, that summer.*

Above: *At first glance not unlike London Transport's own ill-fated Leyland Atlanteans, ERV 247D, working the Round London Sightseeing Tour in Buckingham Palace Road in April, was a hired-in 1966 ex-Portsmouth Atlantean PDR1A/1 with Metro-Cammell bodywork.*

Below: *In red/white to operate LT's day and half-day tours, National Travel (London) BGY 581T, a 1979 AEC Reliance 6U3ZR with Plaxton body, in Parliament Square in April.*

Above: *At Castletown, in July, Isle of Man National Transport no.80, a 1965 Leyland Atlantean PDR1/1 with Metro-Cammell body, formerly Merseyside PTE CKF 736C, one of several Atlanteans bought from 'mainland' operators at that time.*

Left: *In the days when Dennis buses were still fairly rare in the UK, Greater Manchester Transport no.1439, one of two Dominator DDA136 with Northern Counties bodies delivered in 1981. It is seen in Oldham in August.*

Above: *Its proximity to Leyland meant that the Ribble company was used by Leyland to test experimental vehicles. GFR 799W was one of two early National 2s with L11 engines (model NL116690/1R), and joined the Ribble fleet in 1980. It is seen at Wigan in August.*

Below: *Acquired from Leyland Vehicles in 1983, this National 10351B/1R had been on extended loan to Ribble from 1979. No.686 is seen at Burnley in August.*

Above: *Prominently liveried for the X43 Manchester-Burnley express service, Ribble no.1121, a 1980 Leyland Leopard PSU3E/4R with Duple 49-seat body, leaves Burnley bus station in August.*

Below: *Buses can no longer pick up passengers outside Birmingham's Council House, but in September 1982 Colmore Row still led traffic through the city centre. West Midlands Travel no.6302, a 1977 Leyland Fleetline FE30ALR with Metro-Cammell body.*

Above: *Miles from congested urban centres, Morar Motors EST 822E, a 1967 Bedford VAMS with Alexander Y type body, new to Highland Omnibuses, pauses at Morar in May to allow the driver to make a phone call while on service between Mallaig and Fort William.*

Below: *On the Isle of Skye in May, Highland Scottish no.L28, a newly-delivered Leyland Leopard PSU3F/4R with Alexander Y type 62-seat body, drops pupils at Portree High School.*

Above: *Ready for delivery from Duple's Blackpool coachworks in March, a Western Scottish Volvo B10M with Dominant III bodywork in the corporate Scottish blue/white. On the right, Scottish Bus Group chairman, Ian Irwin chats with Duple salesman Eddie Brown.*

Left: *Newly delivered in April to Lothian Region Transport, Leyland Olympian no.666, one of two with Alexander R type bodies, climbs away from Granton, Edinburgh. This bus was prematurely withdrawn in 1987 when it was badly damaged by fire – surely no connection with its fleetnumber?*

Above: *Gleaming in the May sunshine at Lochee depot, two former Dundee Corporation Daimlers preserved by Tayside Region. No.127 is a 1951 CVD6 with Glasgow-built Croft body, and no.184 is a 1955 CVG6 with Metro-Cammell Orion body.*

Below: *Tayside Regional Transport bought five of these Dennis Dominator DDA139 in 1981 with East Lancs bodies, but their stay in Dundee was short. No.284 in seen in May.*

AECs THAT HAD LEYLAND 'HEARTS'

ALAN TOWNSIN tells the story of a secret liaison, even though solemnised in a licensing arrangement, which resulted in the use of Leyland's pot-cavity diesel combustion system of the 1930s in the AEC 8.8-litre engines fitted to large numbers of London Transport AEC buses and coaches, as well as in batches for operators in the north of England, Scotland, Wales and even as far afield as Durban.

FROM 1930 onwards, the development of road transport diesel engines, then more often called oil engines, was very rapid. It was recognised from the start that much depended on the design of the combustion chamber and just where the fuel was injected into the engine. At a meeting of the Municipal Tramways and Transport Association, held in Manchester in September 1931 as the result of the initiative of Stuart Pilcher, perhaps the leading municipal transport general manager of his day, what proved to be the three most successful engine designs of the following years all appeared for the first time.

One was the first engine to use the Ricardo 'Comet' indirect injection system, in which the fuel was injected into a spherical air cell connected to the cylinder by a narrow passage. This was also the first AEC engine in the 8.8-litre series that was to be standard for most oil-engined AEC models until early 1935. It had been developed from the first production AEC oil engine, an 8.1-litre unit using a different Acro air-cell combustion system, introduced in October 1930. The first Comet-head engine had been fitted in great haste in LT643, one of the AEC Renown six-wheeled double-deckers then in production for the London General Omnibus Co Ltd, so that it could be driven to the MTTA meeting. Power curves published at the time showed an output of 130bhp at a remarkable 2,500rpm, though

Previous page: The 10T10 class of Green Line coaches were a familiar part of the London scene from their introduction in 1938 until replaced by their RF-class successors in 1952/3. The construction of their LPTB-built bodywork was described in the trade press when they were new, but there was coyness about the specification of the AEC Regal chassis and never a mention of the fact that their smooth-running 8.8-litre engines had the Leyland-designed pot-cavity combustion system. Seen here just after postwar refurbishing is T684, the view showing that these particular vehicles did not have the pronounced forward projection of the radiator found on most 8.8-litre installations.
London Transport

Above: Another contributor to London Transport's small fleet of oil-engined Leylands was the City Motor Omnibus Co Ltd, taken over in November 1934, whose newest buses were three Titanic TT2 models (the six-wheel equivalent of the TD2) dating from 1933. Despite the remarkably old-fashioned appearance of their 62-seat Dodson bodies, built to a City specification, they were oil-engined from new – AGH 149, seen here not long after entering service as City's no.TS1, became the LPTB's TC1. The oil engines were later removed but it seems that they were fitted to TD-class Titans.
The Omnibus Society

further development allowed production A165 versions to give the same power at a rather more conservative 2,000rpm. It was the most powerful British road transport oil engine of its day, smooth-running although not reaching the fuel economy standards of the better direct-injection units.

Another key engine to make its appearance was the first Leyland oil engine to be put on public display. Leyland had avoided rushing into this line of business and even here only had a prototype six-cylinder engine, of 8.1-litre capacity, running in a lorry, but this design too was a winner. It was a direct-injection engine, the fuel being injected directly into the cylinders, and the shape of the cavity in the top of the piston into which it was injected, very like the inside of a flower pot, proved remarkably successful in giving smooth running – engines of this form were usually described as pot-cavity units. Its output at that stage was quite modest, quoted as 85bhp even though the speed then given, 2,000rpm, was quite high, but even at that initial stage its refined behaviour was being praised.

For the record, the third epoch-making engine to appear at the 1931 MTTA meeting was the first Gardner LW-series engine, a 6LW, with that maker's own very efficient form of direct injection, and, although not directly involved in the current story, that range greatly influenced later bus engine development, indeed playing its part in causing AEC to switch to direct injection.

Kept quiet

The following is the story of how the Leyland pot-

The order for 100 new Leyland Titan TD4 buses delivered to London Transport in 1937 may have been intended partly to accelerate modernisation of the fleet in a Coronation year, but it was also an indication of the Board's willingness to look elsewhere than to AEC for part of its vehicle supplies, as well as an implicit seal of approval for the Leyland pot-cavity engine with which they were fitted. The Leyland metal-framed bodies were to a style intended to resemble the standard Chiswick-built design as then being built for STL-class AECs. STD94 is seen at Hendon a few months after entering service. They proved very successful and, remarkably, the entire batch survived until planned withdrawal began in 1953.
G H F Atkins

cavity principle came to be applied to the AEC 8.8-litre engine, via a licensing agreement yet still kept very quiet indeed, despite the production of quite a large family of buses so powered.

Leyland built only small numbers of its new 8.1-litre engine in 1932, though they earned good reputations, full-scale production not beginning until 1933 – by November that year the power output was being quoted as 87bhp at 1,800rpm, slightly increased but still modest in relation to its size. Meanwhile, the LGOC had 94 AEC-Ricardo 8.8-litre engines, some rebuilt from earlier AEC-Acro engines, in service by November 1932, together with 11 of the Gardner 6LW — the largest oil-engined bus fleet in Britain at the time, all in AEC Renown LT-class double-deckers.

When the London Passenger Transport Board came into being in 1933, its first major decision in regard to bus engineering was to standardise on oil-engined buses. Because the 8.8 was a bulky engine, it was decided initially to convert further LT-class buses, not so tightly limited in dimensions or weight, using the petrol engines released in new four-wheel STL-class AEC Regent buses – 339 of the LT class were thus converted between September 1933 and October 1934. However, AEC was no longer an associated concern, as had been so in LGOC days, and although there was an agreement making AEC the main supplier of motorbuses to the Board for ten years, there was greater freedom to examine alternatives.

Over its first few years, the LPTB took over the other bus fleets in London, adding them to those from the LGOC. Among the independent concerns, the most popular double-decker had been the Leyland Titan, mostly petrol-engined TD1 or in a few cases TD2 models, of which 112 had been taken into the Central Area fleet by 1936. In addition, however, there were a small number of similar buses with the above-mentioned Leyland 8.1-litre oil engine. The first, coming into the London Transport fleet with the business of Birch Bros Ltd in February 1934, was one of the last TD1 buses to be built, GX 131, dating from early 1932, but fitted with an oil engine in June 1933, becoming TD85 in the LPTB fleet. It is ironic that the Birch family, fiercely opposed to the compulsory takeover, should have contributed a bus that was destined to set off a chain reaction

materially influencing London Transport vehicle engine policy in the remainder of the 1930s.

In general, LPTB was seeking to standardise its fleet, so oddities usually received short shrift. It was thus quite remarkable that in addition to this bus remaining in use, four more ex-independent Titans (two TD1 from Westminster Omnibus Co Ltd, a TD2 from The St George Omnibus Co Ltd and a TD1 from Miller Traction Co Ltd, respectively numbered TD94, 95, 98 and 105), acquired in July/August 1934, were converted to diesel by LPTB after takeover, using similar 8.1-litre engines, in October of that year.

Then the City Motor Omnibus Co Ltd was taken over in November, contributing another oil-engined Titan which became TD121 (some records show it, and a few others in this fleet, as a TS3, which was a Tiger model dimensionally similar to the TD1, though others as a TD Special). More impressively, there were also three Titanic TT2 six-wheelers, new in 1933, also oil-engined as received, which were given fleet numbers TC1-3.

Among early provincial users of the A180 pot-cavity engine was Salford Corporation, which took delivery of its first 15 Regents so powered in the latter part of 1938. These retained the usual 8.8-litre installation, with the radiator set about 4^{1}/$_{2}$in further forward than needed for the 7.7-litre engine by then standard – it was also raised and tilted back a little, due to these engines needing to be raised slightly at the front to give adequate clearance, always striking the author as giving a slightly 'snooty' look to such vehicles. No.13 was one of five with Park Royal bodies that dated from October of that year.
Park Royal

The largest group of buses powered by 8.8-litre pot engines ultimately reached nearly 1,000 buses, all but a small minority of the London LT-class AEC Renown six-wheel double-deckers with enclosed-stair bodies built in 1931/2. Most were petrol-engined when new, including LT156, dating from January 1931. It was among 400 buses that received new A180 engines in 1938/9, in this case in October 1938. In the usual London fashion, bodies were transferred between chassis at overhaul and that shown was from a batch built later in 1931 with destination box built into the projecting cab roof. The picture dates from soon after the war when these buses were second only to the STL in terms of numbers in service.
B V Franey

Collection

Thus London Transport thus had built up a collection of nine oil-engined Leylands. At first thought, it might have seemed surprising that the three ex-City Titanics were converted to petrol, but it may be that they had proved rather underpowered with the 87bhp maximum output quoted for the 8.1-litre oil engine at the time. However three more Titans (TD96, a TD1 from the Westminster fleet, and two TD2 models, TD124 from the Reliance Omnibus Co Ltd and TD130 from the Prince Omnibus Co Ltd) became oil in 1935, restoring the total to nine, presumably using the engines removed from the Titanics, so it was clear that the Leyland oil engines continued to be of interest.

This was underlined by the allocation of all nine oil-engined Titans to Hanwell garage, where their performance could be compared with some oil-engined AECs – significantly, this was the closest garage to AEC's works at Southall, only half a mile or so from the main entrance. Records imply that at least one of the engines had been exchanged or rebuilt to

become of the new 8.6-litre size resulting from Leyland's adoption of 4$\frac{1}{2}$in instead of 4$\frac{3}{8}$in bore; this became Leyland's standard six-cylinder oil engine used in most of its range from 1934. Figures for the output of this engine varied, earlier versions usually given as 94bhp, later going to 98bhp, with 1,900rpm governed speed.

London Transport had meanwhile standardised on STL-type AEC buses with that maker's 7.7-litre engine, in those days of type A171 with Ricardo Comet cylinder head, which had gone into large-scale production from late 1934. Even so, the purchase of 100 new oil-engined Titan TD4 buses that formed London Transport's STD class delivered in April-June 1937 gives an indication that the nine Leyland oil engines had formed a good impression. However, even more significant was a test report from AEC's experimental department dated 16 March 1937 showing that an AEC 8.8-litre engine had

The A180 engine as being produced in 1938/9. That shown, number A180C 699, was one of a batch built for AEC Renown model O664 single-deckers for South Wales Transport Co Ltd and used on the arduous Townhill route. The suffix C indicates a pot-cavity engine built to 'provincial' (ie non-London) specification and with fluid flywheel, for use in a bus with preselective transmission, the equivalent engine with clutch for a crash gearbox being of type A180D.
AEC

been converted to the Leyland pot-cavity system with single-hole injector and was giving 'very encouraging results', it being suggested that production of such an engine should be considered.

Strong interest

It is clear that there was strong London Transport interest, for by June 1937 such '8.8 pot' engines were specified for a new fleet of AEC Regal single-deck chassis for Green Line coaches (also part of the LPTB empire) to enter service in 1938. The manufacture of such engines required a licensing agreement with Leyland, and it is interesting to speculate as to the reasons behind the latter's willingness to agree. One factor may have been the amount of business Leyland was obtaining from the LPTB, not only the STDs, the small C-class Cub buses and development work on other new single-deckers but even larger orders for trolleybuses, not covered by the agreement that gave AEC most of the bus chassis work.

Aberdeen Corporation was another user, its no.6 dating from late 1938 being posed for photography at the AEC works before setting off on what looks likely to have been a chilly 500-mile drive north. It was one of five buses with A180C engines and Weymann metal-framed 54-seat bodies.
AEC

Unwillingness to co-operate might have jeopardised Leyland's choice of receiving further business.

Doubtless both AEC and Leyland were embarrassed, for different reasons, for there was no public reference to the manufacture of these engines. As was to be expected, they had characteristics very like the Leyland engines using the same combustion system, and as it happened they were also very similar in size – the Leyland 8.6-litre engine's bore size of $4^1/2$in translates to 114.3mm, compared to the 8.8 engine's 115mm, while the Leyland's $5^1/2$in stroke is equivalent to 139.7mm, whereas the AEC

8.8 stroke was 142mm. References to the A180 pot engine's output varied between 90 and 100bhp, usually at 1,800rpm, as with the Leyland quite a modest figure and well down on the 8.8 Comet engine with its capability of up to 130bhp.

Yet the easy-going way the 8.8 pot engines performed, with smooth and relatively quiet running throughout the speed range, somehow made this seem unimportant – as with the Leyland equivalent, this was so despite the use of very simple mounting, the engines being bolted almost directly into the frame. The AEC engine did not have the deep roar so characteristic of the Leyland, but there was very similar smoothness of running.

Fuel economy was considered sufficiently better by both LPTB and others for 8.8-litre engines to be converted from Comet to pot on quite a large scale. Another factor in this may have been improved starting from cold – the Comet engines needed electric heater plugs and, even with these in use, the process was sometimes difficult in cold weather, and there was a good deal of light-coloured smoke emitted until the engine warmed up.

10T10 coaches

The immediate result were the famous 10T10 Green Line coaches, of which 266 were built, proving popular with passengers, drivers and workshop staff – as with almost all AEC vehicles built for the LPTB in that period, they had fluid flywheels and Wilson-type preselective gearboxes. There had been a previous batch of coaches of generally similar design, the 9T9 type, using the 7.7-litre engine which would actually have been more powerful with their original indirect-injection engines set to the usual 115bhp rating of the time but the 10T10 had a more relaxed easy-going way of covering the ground.

The first few 8.8 pot engines for the 10T10s were designated A165Z but thereafter the general type designation A180 was introduced to cover 8.8-litre direct-injection engines, at that stage all with pot-cavity and bearing a plate recording the licensing arrangement with Leyland. The engines for the 10T10 coaches, type A180A as built, also differed from other 8.8-litre engines in having a more compact front-end design, with no fan and the water pump repositioned so as to minimise the bonnet length but other 8.8 pot engines retained the standard design, with fan, and thus continued to have the characteristic $4^1/_2$in forward projection of the radiator – the front of the engine, and the radiator with it, was also lifted slightly to give adequate clearance within the frame, giving most 8.8-litre AEC buses their characteristic slightly 'snooty' look.

A further 400 conversions of LT-class double-deckers from petrol, this time using 'pot' engines of type A180B as built, were put in hand by the LPTB, these being carried out between August 1938 and April 1939. A last batch of 150 basically similar conversions from petrol were carried out between July 1939 and January 1940, though these had minor changes and were A180G (later the A180M, N or P designations were applied to rebuilds to a similar specification of the main earlier types of LPTB 8.8-litre engines). Thereafter, the only LT-class double-deckers with petrol engines were 149 of the original open-staircase deliveries of 1929/30, plus 54 with fluid flywheel transmission (conversions of the latter too were evidently in mind but never carried out).

Here again, the pot-cavity engines as applied to the LT-class buses proved to be very smooth-running and in one respect were actually slightly superior to the 10T10 coaches in getting the full benefit of the excellent standard of steady almost vibration-free idling that these engines gave. This was because the buses in question all had crash gearboxes and did not

The A180C engine was also chosen by Durban Corporation in South Africa for six Regal single-deckers with Park Royal 39-seat bodies delivered in March-April 1939. They were not subject to home market dimensional limits and had longer and wider bodywork than then allowed in Britain as well as bumpers at front and rear.
Park Royal

Brighton Corporation began bus operation in the spring of 1939 with a fleet of 21 AEC Regent buses having 8.8-litre pot-cavity engines, fluid flywheel transmission and Weymann bodies. In this line-up at the AEC works, the vehicle second from the right is no.63 (FUF 63), which still survives.
AEC

suffer from a tendency to a slight 'surging' effect due to the effect of fluid flywheel drag when idling in gear as experienced at times with the preselector gearbox.

AEC oil engines almost always idled very steadily, doubtless reflecting the importance given to this on a London bus, frequently stationary at stops or in traffic, but the 'pot' engine was smoother and quieter in this respect than either the Comet engine (where there was a 'nasal' combustion noise at tick-over speeds even though this faded out as speed rose) or the toroidal direct injection engine mentioned below, which was slightly rougher-running. An LT with 'pot' engine could be mistaken for a slightly tappety petrol engine, as can still be verified by the preserved example, LT165, and in this respect seemed slightly superior to a Leyland 8.6-litre engine, when there was usually slight unevenness.

Conversions

The final step in the story relating to London Transport was triggered by its engineers' decision to convert all its A165-type Comet-head 8.8-litre engines to the pot-cavity form. This involved the 339 LT-type buses that had been converted from petrol in 1933/4, a further 24 similar conversions made in 1937 (the petrol engines from which had gone into the LTC-class Renown single-deck private-hire

coaches built that year) and 62 buses of the 60-seat 'Bluebird' type that had had A165 engines from new in 1932. With the 12 lowbridge 'Godstone' Regents of 1934 and spare units also included in the exercise, some 488 engines were converted.

The end result of this was that about 975 of the LT-class double-deckers, all but a small minority of those with enclosed-stair bodies built in 1931/2, were running with 8.8 'pot' engines from 1943. With the 10T10 coaches (temporarily out of public use at the time, but reappearing after the war) and others, there were thus up to about 1,250 of these engines in use within London Transport's fleet, second in numbers only to the 7.7-litre engines found in the STL class etc.

Other customers

What seems even more surprising in retrospect was that the A180 pot engine had meanwhile become available to other AEC customers. Although the 7.7-litre engine had been standard for most models

since 1935, some operators continued to specify the 8.8-litre, initially in A165 Ricardo Comet-head form. Some did so because there was a continued need for the extra power, but others favoured the larger engine more for reasons of engine durability, and the A180 may have appealed to some of these on grounds of its better fuel economy. How the word got round that such an engine was available is not clear, for there was no mention in the trade press nor, so far as I've ever seen, any publicity, though in the case of municipal fleets it may have been offered in response to invitations to tender and doubtless by direct contact with major operators.

New buses with A180 pot-cavity engines were supplied from mid-1938 to 1939 or in a few cases up to 1941 to the municipal fleets of Aberdeen (five Regent), Brighton (21 Regent), Dundee (four Regent, evidently supplied as A165 but converted within a year), Rochdale (five Regent), Salford (35 Regent and five Regal), Sheffield (at least 19 Regent) and a small number for Halifax, though there the emphasis continued to be on power and there were experiments to go beyond the 130bhp available from the A165

Rochdale Corporation was another municipal operator in the north of England to nominate the A180C engine as its choice. The choice of bodybuilder, Eastern Coach Works Ltd, produced an unusual combination. No.160 was one of five Regents dating from March 1939.
ECW

version. Most had fluid flywheel transmission, these engines being largely A180C though Salford favoured the crash gearbox, the equivalent engine type then being A180D. In addition, two BET-group companies had examples; the South Wales Transport Co Ltd had 13 Renown six-wheel single-deckers with A180C engines, fluid transmission being chosen for its arduous Townhill route in Swansea, and the Rhondda Transport Co Ltd had 17 Regals, including three coaches, these having crash gearboxes. There was also at least one export order, Durban Corporation in South Africa having six Regals of this type with fluid transmission early in 1939.

From early in 1939, AEC itself was standardising on direct-injection engines of a different type, with toroidal (or broadly-speaking 'doughnut-shaped')

The 13 South Wales single-deckers built in 1939 on AEC Renown chassis with 8.8-litre pot engines and fluid transmission had Brush 39-seat bodywork. This view of CWN 395 dates from postwar, by which date its fleetnumber was 43 instead of the original 195, but the view conveys their appearance as built in most respects, though it seems that the slim spacing panel on the offside of the radiator had been removed.
C J Taylor collection

piston cavity, the 7.7-litre A173 version already being in production by then. It gave improved fuel consumption, becoming regarded as even more important when war was declared in September 1939. A toroidal version of the 8.8-litre A180 engine was introduced from about mid-1939, those for bus use mostly having suffix letters A180J (crash) or A180K (fluid), and generally these displaced the pot-cavity version in production, several of the municipal fleets which had 'pot' engines in service switching to the toroidal version for later batches of buses, and there were fresh customers, notably Sydney, which took 43 Regents with the A180J in 1939/40. However, London Transport continued to favour the pot-cavity engine, even adopting the idea for the 9.6-litre engines, type A185, in the first production batch of RT-type buses, numbered RT2-151, placed in service from 1940.

Municipal fleets

Conversions of A165 Comet-head engines in municipal fleets also became quite common. For example, Bradford Corporation's fleet of 25 Regents dating from early 1935 and so powered as built were converted to A180, the engine numbers suggesting that they would have been pot-cavity at that stage at least. Most or all of the 8.8-litre Regents in the Nottingham fleet were converted to A180 specification and it seems probable that this may also have applied to many, possibly most, other municipal or BET-group users of 8.8-litre engines in

vehicles that were expected to remain in service for a sufficient number of years to make it worth while. Later conversions were usually to toroidal and, remarkably, Rochdale proceeded to convert its pot-cavity engines to toroidal as early as September 1940.

AEC practice was to give serial numbers to each major engine type in a series beginning at 1, with a single series for A180 variants (both pot and toroidal), which included both new and converted engines, the latter generally receiving new numbers on conversion. The indications are that a total of about 1,700 8.8-litre direct-injection engines existed, and as some engines were converted by operators, with varying practice in terms of renumbering, or by AEC Service Depots which used a separate numbering series, the total might have been higher. Many such buses ran well into the post-war period, and in a few cases into the 1960s, a handful surviving into preservation.

In London, the oil-engined LT-class buses remained in full-time everyday service through the war years, many important routes being operated by

Rhondda Transport Co Ltd had 17 Regals with similar engines, though these had crash gearboxes, and bodywork by Weymann, the buses being to that operator's standard rear-entrance design of the time. Three were 31-seat coaches to the unusual style seen in this view of no.161 in the original blue and cream livery when new in February 1939.
C J Taylor collection

them exclusively, only a few casualties of wartime air raids having been withdrawn up to 1947. At the end of May in that year, the number of all LT-class double-deckers licensed was 1,184, or 96.9% of the total number of such vehicles built between 1929 and 1932, which included the early open-staircase petrol examples. Taking the class as a whole, they were among the oldest buses in the fleet and very obviously outdated in body style although the bodies on the 1931 buses seemed solidly built, yet the 8.8 pot engines fitted to most made them quite efficient buses. Their performance could best be described as 'stately', but they ran smoothly and were much more pleasant buses in which to ride than, say, the utility Guy Arabs with Gardner five-cylinder engines which seemed to make much heavier weather of the full passenger loads which were then usual, certainly at rush hours.

High standard

The 10T10 coaches were refurbished to a high standard after returning from war duties (some had been used as rather superior mobile canteens called 'Clubmobiles' for the US Air Force) and again became the mainstay of the Green Line services, not seeming at all outdated until replaced by the underfloor-engined RF coaches in 1951/2; some then continued on bus duties for a further year or two. The regard for them by the generation who remembered them in service was fully comparable to that later earned by the RF.

The survival rate of municipal or company fleets of 8.8-litre buses into the postwar era varied. Most of those running in any quantity after 1948 were direct-

injection either as built or by conversion. Some had long lives, up to 20 years or more, especially where fitted with good-quality metal-framed bodies. The four Dundee Regents of 1938 remained in service until 1957, for example, while the five in Aberdeen of 1939 were withdrawn in 1959. At Brighton, eight of the 21 of 1939 were still in service in 1963, and the writer recalls how their sound effects as they passed in the street echoed those of the 10T10s to which they were close cousins in mechanical design. Happily, the famous FUF 63 from the Brighton batch survives, thanks to Mike Dryhurst and in more recent years the considerable efforts in engine rebuilding of Tim Nicholson and Jonathan Pye.

I have always found this family of AECs particularly appealing, not least because the lack of publicity on their engine design has often made them an under-appreciated species. I am grateful to Gordon Baron, Philip Groves, Gavin Martin, Tim Nicholson, Harry Pick and Brian Thackray for help in piecing together this hitherto largely untold story. Some of the more technical aspects were covered in an article I wrote for the April 1999 issue of *AEC Society Gazette*. **CB**

CB YEARBOOK 7 INCLUDED AN ARTICLE ON GREEN LINE DOUBLE-DECKERS BY CHRIS DREW, ILLUSTRATED WITH HIS LINE DRAWINGS. THIS LED TO A SERIES IN CB MAGAZINE ON LONDON VEHICLE TYPE LETTERS THAT HAVE BEEN USED MORE THAN ONCE – USUALLY ON VERY DIFFERENT BUSES

TOUGH GUYS

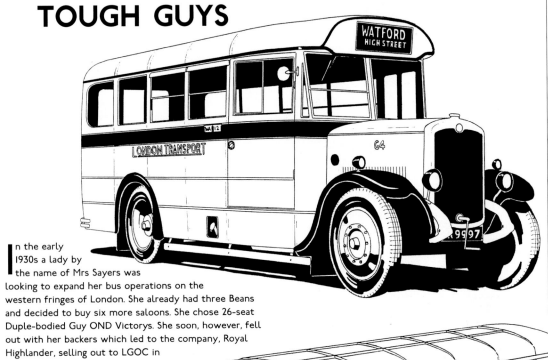

In the early 1930s a lady by the name of Mrs Sayers was looking to expand her bus operations on the western fringes of London. She already had three Beans and decided to buy six more saloons. She chose 26-seat Duple-bodied Guy OND Victorys. She soon, however, fell out with her backers which led to the company, Royal Highlander, selling out to LGOC in September 1932, whereafter the Guys were classified G.

London's standard wartime bus was the G, the chassis a Guy Arab, simple and hard-wearing. A total of 435 Gs were built during and just after the troubles, being bodied by five different builders to basic utility designs. As with other utilities, it was the bodywork that was to let them down and shorten their London lives. They were all gone by the early 1950s but some were rebodied by second owners and went on to give many years of useful service. There was one more Guy in the class, G436. This was to be considered as Guy's answer to the RT. (Now, there's a couple of letters I bet will never be used again!)

BUSES AND BELFRIES

One of Robert Jowitt's earliest bus photographs – taken in 1959 on a folding Kodak 620 roll-film camera – depicting a 1957 East Midland Leyland PD3/4 with Weymann lowbridge body passing the celebrated twisted spire of St Mary and All Saints, Chesterfield. All photos by Robert E Jowitt

In August 1964 the trolleybus wires are still up and the trolleybuses are still running – just! – but here we see a nearly-new replacing Leyland Atlantean/Weymann passing the Cathedral in Newcastle-upon-Tyne.

ROBERT E JOWITT does not consider that he is bats about buses, or not many buses anyway – even if he is about trams – and he here indicates, in perhaps rather more serious vein than usual, that his mind can dwell on higher matters, both architectural and on the implications contained behind the vast diversity of ecclesiastical façades

MY CHIEF CLAIM to fame – if such it be – as a bus photographer lies undoubtedly in the field of taking pictures of buses with girls; to the extent, my detractors may rightly argue, of considering the girl more important than the bus. In fairness to myself, however, I must state that I have used many other themes to enhance buses which on their own might prove pretty boring; and not least among these themes has been architecture, both secular and ecclesiastical. For verily the architecture past which the bus travels is part of the life of that bus; a bus among the flowery Victorian villas on the South Coast will look very different from its identical sister traversing grimy terraces of the industrial North . . . or ditto ditto the thatched cottages of East Anglia versus the miners' homes of the Welsh Valleys.

In order to 'set the record straight' and to prove that buses complete with girls are not the only expression of my art, I propose in these next few pages to dwell upon the delights of buses with an architectural backdrop – or, as my detractors might say, buses with an excessive amount of building in relation to the bus – and moreover, in this case, I will limit myself to the ecclesiastical side of the matter . . . for to tackle the whole field of architectural backgrounds to buses would occupy all the pages of this book, and then some!

Fortunate

I am fortunate perhaps that I learned the orders of

With Ford products to the fore, Jowitt's notes unfortunately failed to record the exact location of this fine Tudor-looking tower and classical façade in 1961 (probably January) with what would now be regarded as equally classic street furniture and a 1939 AEC/MCW L1 class chassisless trolleybus heading towards Liverpool Street station, London.

This Lothian Leyland Olympian/ECW coming up Edinburgh's Royal Mile past the steeple of the Tron Kirk in 1999 may in the course of time and even fairly soon be esteemed as a classic bus. Meanwhile the Lothian & Borders Fire Brigade is busy dealing with a bomb scare in the City Chambers.

English ecclesiastical architecture at about the same time that I learned to read and write. My father in his young days had an architectural training and was for some years employed by what was then known as the Ministry of Works (now English Heritage) as recorder of finds during the excavation and restoration of various ruined abbeys and other sites in the 1920s, and he made sure that from my cradle onwards I could tell the difference between Norman, Early English, Decorated, Perpendicular and so forth; thus this knowledge or information is far more deeply rooted in my subconscious than the later acquired recognition of the difference between, for

example, an RM and an RML. And to this knowledge, as years passed by, I have added as a matter of course and without really thinking about it the recognition, as and when I encountered them, of such foreign types as Austrian Baroque and Portuguese Manueline. Thus not only has it been a joy but also an instinct to add the full height of some florid tower to the photograph of the bus, even if the bus pales almost into insignificance at the foot of the tower.

My first essay in bus and church photography is now more than 40 years ago. At that date I had no interest in photographing buses (except perhaps

The Chausson served faithfully in many French cities in various forms from the immediate postwar years until the early 1970s. A typical example is here parked immediately below the twin towers of Orleans Cathedral in 1969.

derelict veterans on fairgrounds) for I was entirely devoted (and quite rightly in my opinion) to photographing trams, but it so happened that my father and I, *en route* to trams in Sheffield, paused in Chesterfield which is famed for the twisted spire of its church (St Mary and All Saints, the spire being late C14th, 228ft high). Trams in Chesterfield were in the late 1950s long since dead and gone, so perforce the photo of the crooked spire had to be improved by – in the terms of that era – a fairly common bus.

If that particular bus was no better than boring there were plenty more meritorious cases, especially when it came to trolleybuses which were always for me more desirable than most (though not all) motorbuses. In Derby, for example, the tower of All Saints (early c16th) loomed impressively above the

double wires, and in Bournemouth high Victorian specimens soared heavenward, notably the tower of St Stephen's (1881-98, architect Pearson, though the tower actually was supervised by Pearson's son in 1907 and a spire remained merely an intention) above route 25 breasting the summit of Poole Hill and the spire of St Peter's (1869-79, architect G E Street) overlooking routes 21, 22, 23, and 24 descending Old Christchurch Road, a mixture of late 1930s Sunbeams, 1950s BUTs and 1959/60 Sunbeam MF2Bs. Could I resist, in such circumstances, from

humming to myself that well-known children's hymn Jesus wants me for a Sunbeam . . . In Newcastle-upon-Tyne matters were even better, for the trolleybuses passed the Cathedral (St Nicholas, c1435) with the curious 'crown' on its tower, though it has to be admitted that this church was not established as a cathedral until 1878 and that the writer of Methuen's red guide in 1916 considered the building, apart from the tower, 'unimposing and parochial'. I might have said even worse about the Atlanteans, which in the 1960s were replacing the trolleybuses . . .

Parochial

The term 'parochial' has actually some relevance so far as the photography of buses and cathedrals is concerned. The immediate accessibility of Newcastle Cathedral to public transport is indeed on account of the fact that it was formerly a parish church and not a cathedral. Most or many of England's parish churches are placed boldly by the public highway. Suffolk, Norfolk, Lincolnshire, Oxfordshire and the Cotswolds abound in magnificent specimens of parish churches which at one time – and perhaps some of them even now – would form brilliant adjuncts to classic bus photographs. I have heard, on

Above left: In Osnabrück in 1963 an intrepid cyclist (moto-aided) overtakes a one-and-a-half deck trolleybus, typical of that period in both trolleybus and motorbus forms in many German systems.

Above: *Unsung in guidebooks but entirely Austrian in architectural inspiration with the onions crowning its tower is this church in Klagenfurt, seen not long after Saurer diesel buses – and trailers – had replaced the trolleybuses in the summer of 1963.*

the other hand, that Stow-on-the-Wold, for example, has these days no bus services at all, classic or otherwise. In the case of the genuine pre-Reformation cathedral, however, as opposed to those new dioceses which were created to cope with the Industrial Revolution spread of population (eg Newcastle hived off from Durham, or Guildford and Portsmouth hacked out of Winchester) the cathedrals themselves are as a general rule tucked away in a close which both spiritually and architecturally forbids any close contact from public service vehicles. (I wonder how even dustcarts can manage

includes St Giles', can claim an architecture both secular and ecclesiastical which, as 'the Athens of the north', must put it high on any bus photographer's list even if the charm of the girls straying along Princes Street is hard to abandon . . . And, despite modernity sweeping in, Edinburgh seems to manage to retain quite a lot of buses which can be counted as classic . . . Further exceptions to the rule are, of course, St Paul's and Westminster Abbey (though the purist in matters ecclesiastical may argue that Westminster is not a cathedral) and these two are so frequently reproduced with RTs and RMs as decorative adjuncts on picture postcards that I do not believe I have ever bothered to photograph them myself . . .

On the Continent matters seem to me to be arranged more satisfactorily – ie more like St Giles' and St Paul's – with not only parish churches but also cathedrals closely flanked by trams, trolleybuses or buses. I regret I have never researched into why this should be, why foreign cathedrals are not on the whole sheltered by closes; it would be an interesting subject to pursue, if life were long enough . . . and there weren't so many buses and girls to pursue . . .

Apart from my reputation in the area of buses plus girls I can claim – justifiably, I feel – some fame as a recorder of the buses of Paris . . . in the days when many if not most were still petrol-engined Renaults with the celebrated open rear platform. These vehicles were, in my eyes, almost alone among buses, so marvellous as to stand on their own merits for photographic purposes without the addition of any props, but naturally I used a lot of the architectural delights of Paris as well, and not least its churches, Notre Dame *y inclus*.

Gallic charms

Elsewhere in France the cathedrals of Metz, Orleans and La Rochelle, to name but three, were hemmed

to penetrate some of those narrow little gateways!) Durham Cathedral, perched on a crag above the river, is almost impossible anyway, Winchester, with the longest nave in England, can only be tackled by ascending the hills in the vicinity and using it either as incidental detail in the background or dragging it up with a telephoto lens, York can likewise serve only as the distant scene, Exeter is a 'non-starter', and even Salisbury, with the tallest spire in England, at 404ft, requires careful manipulation, even if some of the buses which visit the city on market days from outlying villages could until recent years and perhaps even today claim to be classic . . . or at least ex-Londoners. I will leave the positions of the rest of the English cathedrals to the opinions of those readers who live in their vicinity (Norwich, spire second only to Salisbury at 315ft, Lincoln, one-time-home to a fleet of delectable Leyland Tiger Cubs if there was anything you could do with them in these circumstances) and so on . . . while feeling bound to add (for the sake of the Scottish Editor of this book) that if you would take a trip north of the border you would find that St Giles' Cathedral, Edinburgh, with a 'crown' upon its tower (apparently of slightly later date than that of Newcastle – to which it may be compared) provided a location for bus-plus-cathedral photography second to none. In point of fact Edinburgh's 'Royal Mile', that street which

about with Chaussons, those buses which were so typically French as to be counted as classic almost from the moment they took the road (I have hymned their charms in the pages of *Buses Yearbook* before now) and as unmistakably Gallic as the soaring towers below which they parked. Then the later generation of Saviem Standards clustered around the carved saints on holy portals, the Saviems so horridly new as seriously to upset my sensibilities . . . though, as diligent readers of *Buses Yearbook* will know, I learned to love them – the buses, I mean, not the readers – and they are now accepted as classic buses in their own right, with examples in preservation. How time passes!

In Germany it was mostly trams (not allowed in these pages) which hugged the precincts of holy ground; or maybe my predilection for trams made me tend to ignore the buses . . . not but what I recall choice spots where trolleybuses, including the curious Teutonic one-and-a-half decker, plied in close proximity to an odour of sanctity. In Austria the same tramway case applied, except in places where trams had been scrapped and the churches – of almost excessively exuberant Baroque – were so irresistible that buses had to serve the purpose. In Switzerland, on the other hand, there were plenty of trolleybuses, and the church architecture was as much Swiss – and could only be Swiss – as that in Austria could only be Austrian, just like Austrian buses and Swiss trolleybuses could be nothing but Austrian and Swiss. The only exception to this was a very Italian trolleybus in Innsbruck, looking very odd in such Baroque and Tyrolean surroundings.

If Alpine specimens of Baroque reached their own heights of superlative I could argue that the heights of Iberian ecclesiastical architecture reached higher . . . in flights of florid nature, frequently, as well as literally from ground level upwards. As for the vehicles passing on ground level, there were occasions when these were quite as exotic and bizarre as their Alpine counterparts were as regimented in design as might be expected of Central European inspiration. The Spanish indigenous Pegaso appeared in two halfcab versions, both nearside and offside cabs (as readers of Buses Annual back numbers may recall) which looked delightfully quaint with a background of the magnificence of Burgos Cathedral. The interior of Burgos Cathedral, incidentally, housed a portrait, attributed to Leonardo da Vinci, of La Magdalena clad in nothing but a vast waterfall of golden curls which provided a serious distraction from even the Pegasos. As for Zaragoza, it could boast two cathedrals, La Seo,

1119-1520 with a tower completed c1686, uncompromisingly austere but grandly so, and Nuestra Senora del Pilar, begun in 1681, with a number of domes and four corner towers, excessively florid, which were part of the original plan but not completed until the C20th towers, both churches well fringed with native Spanish trolleybuses and ex-London Transport Q1s, all in brilliant silver, not to speak (which we mustn't here!) of a gloriously dilapidated collection of thoroughly Spanish trams including picturesque articulated varieties.

Melting wax

Somewhat more sophisticated trams rumbled below the extraordinary pile of the Catalan-Art-Nouveau-Baroque (spires like dripping candles!) cathedral of the Sagrada Familia in Barcelona designed by Antonio Gaudi, an architect renowned also for several *fin de siècle* fantasies in domestic architecture with more melting wax. I think that buses passed the Sagrada Familia too but seem to have failed to photograph them (I wonder why?) so perhaps I should not mention this edifice either, irresistible though it be . . .

Conspicuous

Perhaps, however, this is enough of Spanish idiosyncrasies. We will cross the border into Portugal with its Edwardian-American trams and its 1950s and 1960s mirror-image British double-deck buses, all of them well hymned in previous Jowitt pages; but in these present pages it is the churches behind the vehicles which are under consideration, even while the merit of the vehicles themselves is surely excuse for another glance at them! On the Lisboa bus and tram system the most conspicuous churches are, probably, the Hieronymite monastery at Belém, the Basilica of Estrela, and the Sé or Cathedral on the famous Graça tramline and the fringes of the infamous Alfama quarter. The architectural student not influenced by the transport network might well select other buildings, and these three I have selected in fact have charms almost as paradoxical as those of the wrong-side open-platform and halfcab Weymann-bodied AEC Regent IIIs which terminated at the first two churches and the Regal IIIs which screeched dangerously on the downhill bends past the Sé; for the boldest feature of the monastery at Belém, the tower, is actually only a C19th imitation, while all the most exciting Manueline sections (C15-16th, with borrowings from late Gothic and Moorish) are inside and not visible from buses or trams, and the Basilica of Estrela with two lofty towers on its façade and a huge dome behind (dating merely from 1779-96 and all you would expect of that period) actually contained – somewhere in its upper reaches below the dome – an office which in Salazar or early post-Salazar days was the only place where you could obtain Portuguese ordnance survey maps and with the closest scrutiny of your passport and suspicious assessment of your general character, and even the Cathedral, though it retains its two massively defensive western towers (1380, following earthquake damage in 1344 to the original building founded in 1150 possibly on the site of a mosque) glowering over the bus and tram route, apparently lost most of the rest of its more historic features in the celebrated 1755 earthquake.

In Bilbao, on the opposite side of the neck of Spain, more Q1s, in London Transport red, congregated in the tree-lined square of Arenal, hard by the church of San Nicolás de Bari, 1743, described in the Blue Guide as 'large but uninteresting', with two squat towers capped by domes, while inside, according to an English translation of a local guide book, could be found five alters. While on the subject of translation I might add that should you have travelled on a Q1 to churches elsewhere in Bilbao you would, when you wished to alight, ring a familiar-looking bell inscribed PUSH ONCE. In Spanish this is pronounced – more or less – puss onsay, but the trouble is that in Spanish *once* is the word for eleven; a situation with potential for sending the driver mad . . . Bilbao's finest church is Santiago (mainly c14th and 15th with later additions, a cathedral since 1950) but if you wished to visit this your best bet was a French trolleybus – in London Transport red – with its Vetra front end and windscreen of wistful Gallic expression chopped off and replaced by an unsightly Basque creation. Of the porch of Santiago the local guide book states that it employees the vault-supporting theory . . . and that this includes two potential counter-supports . . . It certainly appears sturdier – and more elegant – than the Vetras did!

After that very long sentence – as A A Milne said in one of those stories – I am now very tired, and as furthermore I have managed to get away with possibly the longest sentence I have ever written for *Classic Bus* without the computer underlining it in green as incoherent I shall now beat a retreat to Porto.

Paradoxical pleasures

Porto, as I have implied already above, and as I have praised previously in past pages of this and similar erudite publications, is another of those paradises with paradoxical transport pleasures such as Latin-American or Belgian-type trams and offside British buses. As for the churches of Porto, the most

It is probably the case, in this 1976 shot of the eastern half of the joint chapels of Carmelitas and Carmo in Porto, that Jowitt's best efforts in the darkroom at correcting ecclesiastical converging verticals failed to take into account the resultant slightly squiffy appearance of the Dalfa-bodied Leyland Atlantean. It is probably equally true that Jowitt on a diet of port wine would see Atlanteans looking just so . . .and wouldn't care, for they were too new to be worth noticing, while the tram was of a far older vintage than any port wine Jowitt ever encountered.

With the onslaught of Godlessness, even in the 1960s, many churches and chapels were proving 'surplus to requirements' and we have here a specimen of ecclesiastical demolition (denomination unknown) encountered in 1964 by this Wolverhampton 1947 Sunbeam F4 with 1960 Roe body on the Walsall-Wolverhampton trolleybus route operated jointly by both towns.

noteworthy – again from the point of view of the traveller on public transport – were – and presumably still are, even in a non-tramway and non-British-bus era – firstly the Clerigos, with Portuguese Baroque bell tower completed in 1763 rising splendidly above the awful tramway gradient out of the Praça da Liberdade, and, not far away, the adjoining chapels of the Carmelitas (C17th) and Carmo (C18th Baroque) but to these must be added any number of churches more or sometimes less visible from public transport, in particular the Cathedral, well served by trolleybus if you could pick your way on foot through notable slums for the last lengths of the visit, and the church of São Francisco if you could suffer the horrid Volvo buses which had replaced the trams in that vicinity and which in retrospect and especially when seen secondhand with operators of fringe-to-central-urban routes won an impulsive if revolting attraction. And among that 'any number' mentioned above several, probably unsung in the guidebooks, offered a backdrop of *azulejo* (or decorative blue-tiled-clad walls) to not only Volvos but also to AECs and Lancia double-deck trolleybuses.

São Fransisco, while offering a fairly undramatic exterior, could claim, within its walls, some of the most fantastic carved and gilded altars you could wish to behold. The church itself is mostly late C14th, the altars C17-18th.

In point of fact the case of glorious interior decorations, whether the exterior be lowly and humble or arch-flamboyant, applies anywhere from the Douro to the'Danube, with divine carvings reminiscent of but far exceeding in their beauty the most decorative of C19th fairground roundabout ornamentation.

If, for a moment, the screeching din of trams and buses becomes too much, if the clatter – or contents – of glasses on café terraces becomes too much, then, perhaps, this is time to seek a moment's tranquility before these devastatingly lovely images to thank whatever Providence as suits your belief for enjoying the good fortune of being in such a place . . .

Non-conformist

The truth is, of course, that all these wondrously ornamented places of worship belong to the Roman Catholic faith. What did we lose in England at the Reformation? It is on record, I believe, that Thomas Cromwell's minions, having launched a vicious attack on the more idolatrous details of Winchester

A classic item – though on the small scale compared with some – of non-conformist 'industrial revolution' architecture at Crows-an-Wra, Cornwall, is accosted by a choice Western National Bristol LWL6B in July 1965. The damsel between the vintage coaching milepost and the ancient cross is a Jowitt importation.

Cathedral and having elected to include the organ in this category – and duly demolished it – then strayed through the streets of Winchester individually 'tootling upon the pipes'. It would be pleasant, but probably too fanciful, to imagine that this piece of barbarity so influenced the citizens of Winchester that a few centuries later they remained devoted, against a 'National' onslaught, to their own King Alfred Motor Services. Anyway, whatever we lost at the Reformation, what we gained instead didn't seem too different to a lot of people, and a lot of people were not any happier. In such an essay as this I cannot dwell upon the rise of the non-conformist churches, save only to speak of their buildings. Blossoming in the main at the height of the Industrial Revolution these buildings – numerous indeed on account of the several divisions and sects of non-conformity – bore a close resemblance to the factory and mill architecture of the period, with a tendency to round-headed windows. Referring to the admittedly grim aspect of some or many of them (you could count, from a Manx Electric tram, half a dozen when passing the more-or-less derelict Isle of Man Road Services depot at Laxey with more-than-less derelict Thornycrofts contained therein) an architecturally inclined and middle-of-the-road C of E friend of my father's exclaimed 'I don't know how they manage to keep any spiritual life alive in such places!'

I do not think this judgement is strictly fair – though alas in changing times with a tendency towards apathetic agnosticism or worse all too many of these chapels are now derelict or converted to heaven-knows-what unsuitable purposes – for, in their heyday, as a study of C19th hymnology will reveal, their walls echoed with some of the most stirring and resounding hymns, by virtue of both words and tunes, ever to grace a printed page. Anyway, architecturally or spiritually forbidding as they might be, and even if or when alternative misuse had set in, they provided striking landmarks which a bus-and-architecture photographer could not ignore.

Perhaps at this juncture I should state, for the benefit of any readers who may wish to know, that while my ancestors included Quakers, Catholics and Jews as well as zealous members of the Established Church it was in this latter that I was brought up; slightly on the low side of it, for my father held in abhorrence all High Anglican practices, deeming them as bad as if not worse than Popery. It was not so much perversity, I think, as sheer mischance, when I was young and frequently in love, that the object of my devotions was all too frequently a Catholic, much to the chagrin of my father. In truth involvement with Catholic girls at that date could prove a bitter business in emotional terms, what with priestly interference and so on, and there were times when I agreed well enough with my father in his quoting of that long-abandoned passage in the Litany: 'From the Bishop of Rome and all his detestable enormities Good Lord Deliver us.' There have been times when I have wondered, since, what this really cost me. Besides which I have never found it easy to choose which provides the greatest inspiration . . . a soul-stirring *tempo di marcia* hot-gospel hymn or the golden angels and sweetly smiling Blessed Virgins of a Papist Iberian or Alpine altar (or even an alter!) any more than I have been able to decide whether it was the 1930s Parisian Renaults or the 1900s Lisbon trams which I truly loved the best. Or Mary or Felicity or Carol or Sally . . . But whatever the future might have been, I have little doubt I would have travelled just the same from Baroque to Baptist, from Büssing to Bristol, from Popery to Prelacy and Saviem to Saurer. It is certainly easier, however, even if lesser fare so far as the soul in concerned, not to think about the religious connotations, just to photograph the towers and spires and belfries . . . and the buses . . . and sometimes the girls . . . but essential none the less to retain somewhere in the back of my mind John Donne's famous words: Never send to know for whom the bell tolls; it tolls for thee! **CB**

No.2: Cardiff Corporation Transport

Born: 1902, when the Cardiff Tramways Company's horse cars were taken over. These services were electrified and were phased out between 1942 and 1950.

Were they replaced by motorbuses?: Not immediately. Trolleybuses, of which more later, took their place, but motorbuses had been operated from Christmas Eve, 1920. The first six were Tilling-Stevens petrol-electrics. Dennises were also operated, as well as Commers and a make called Palladium. By 1928, Cardiff could claim to have the largest municipally owned petrol-engined bus fleet in Britain. By 1931, it was running Albions, Bristols and Thornycrofts in what, for many years, would be one of the most varied fleets in the country.

Did things settle down?: Quite a lot. It bought some Leyland Titans and Tigers and then turned to AECs during the 1930s, while a local connection ensured that most bodywork came from Northern Counties – even though its factory was in far-off Wigan.

What was this curious connection?: That a South Wales family owned Northern Counties, which had its registered office in Cardiff.

And then came trolleybuses?: Yes. Their arrival, in March 1942, was delayed by the outbreak of World War 2, but the AEC and AEC-built BUT three-axle trolleys (including some rare single-deckers) ushered out the trams, only for their own demise to come 20 years after the last tram. The corporation had planned to buy Leyland trolleys, as it had reverted to Leyland buses by then, but Leyland was diverted from buses to military work. But it was able to get them with Northern Counties bodywork and a few other unusual features like two doors and a seated conductor. The trolleybus system survived until January 1970.

What about postwar buses?: They were nothing if not varied and seemed to be dictated by two factors: a desire to support local bodybuilders and acceptance of the most competitive quote for chassis. It's hard to see any other reason why the city would have given itself such a variety of suppliers.

Who did it support?: It turned its bodybuilding allegiance to a company that actually employed people in the city. Air Dispatch (Coachbuilders) Ltd, which like many aircraft companies was able to stave off closure by diverting into meeting the temporary boom in demand for buses, won a contract in 1946 to rebuild some prewar AEC Regents, using parts supplied by East Lancs. It then won orders to assemble East Lancs body parts on new Cardiff chassis, changed its name to Bruce Coachworks and closed in 1951. East Lancs succeeded in retaining much of Cardiff's subsequent business, but 15 Guy Arab IVs were bodied by D J Davies of Treforest in 1953.

But the chassis weren't Welsh?: Sadly, that's one area in which Wales hasn't become renowned, so Cardiff seemed to go out and buy whatever was available for the best price, and that occasionally meant buying bodies from other bodybuilders.

What were these varied buses?: There were AEC Regent IIs, IIIs and Vs, six Crossley DD42/5s, 10 Daimler CVD6s and six CSG6s, the only 20 Bristol KW6Gs ever built, various Arab IVs and Vs, Leyland PD2s, PD3s, Royal Tigers and Tiger Cubs, six AEC Bridgemasters, some Swifts, Daimler Fleetlines and Bristol VRs. And it went on to buy Leyland Olympians, Volvo Ailsas, Seddon midibuses and Leyland Nationals. Other than East Lancs, there were bodies by Alexander (starting with the Crossleys), Northern Counties, Longwell Green, Metro-Cammell Weymann, Willowbrook, Park Royal, ECW and Seddon.

Buses to be cherished, then?: Some should have been, and a few came with registration numbers that would be cherished if they were still around today. We can't help thinking that the plates on CVD6s EBO 1-10 and Crossley EBO 900 of 1948/9 would probably have fetched more today than all those buses cost to buy.

How were these buses painted?: For many years, a combination of cream and crimson lake in traditional municipal style with corporation crests and gold lining. Paint shortages meant some wartime trolleybuses and diesels were grey for a while. All that changed in the early 1970s with a switch to brash orange and white and bilingual fleetnames. That evolved later to incorporate brown as well, but what by then was a council-owned company changed its identity again in 1999 – opting for what's officially described as blue, cream and orange, even if most eyes believe the blue is nearer green.

Alan Millar

Like many municipal operators, Cardiff rebuilt its utility bodies in the early postwar years. This 1946 Bristol K6A with rebuilt Duple bodywork is seen in 1958.
Michael Dryhurst

COACHWORK BY STRACHANS

GEOFF BURROWS
takes a brief look at the history of
one of the well-known coachbuilders of the
20th century with photographs and advertisements
rescued from its archives

IN 1908 James Marshall Strachan opened a coachbuilding and engineering workshop in Netherwood Road, Shepherds Bush, London. All types of manufacture and repairs were undertaken, and by 1911 the work had outgrown the space available. New premises were acquired, at Park Royal (Cumberland Avenue) and Kensington (High Street).

These moves allowed Strachan to graduate towards the manufacture of larger vehicles, and in 1912 the first double-deck bus bodies were constructed, for the Vanguard company. Chars-a-banc followed in 1913, leading to orders for the then new-fangled motorcoaches in 1914. The Great War put a stop to all that, but the expertise of the fledgling company was soon put to good use with the manufacture of aircraft. All production was then moved to even larger premises at Abingdon Road, Kensington. The end of the war in 1918 spelt disaster for a number of companies that had been involved in war work, but at Strachans bodybuilding was rapidly resumed, helping to replace the large numbers of buses which had been sent to the western front and destroyed.

With great confidence for the future, a site was bought in Wales Farm Road, Acton, where the company built a new factory, largely using its own labour force. This was gradually brought into use, and the building was completed in 1921. By 1922, all work had been transferred to the new factory, the last facility to move being the sawmill, after which the Kensington works was vacated.

Innovative

At about this time, W E Brown joined the company. Until now, Strachan himself had been the driving force, but while he was a clever and innovative engineer, he needed somebody to sell the products. Brown proved to be a sales genius, which gave

For all types of metal or composite coachwork consult **STRACHANS**

STRACHANS
SUCCESSORS LTD.

WALES FARM ROAD, NORTH ACTON, LONDON, W.3.

Telephone : ACORN 1851.

Telegrams : STROBUS, PHONE, LONDON.

Strachan time to develop his ideas. Indeed, he set up a new company at this stage so that his development costs could be seen separately from the coachbuilding activities. This was JMS Engineering, and amongst his designs was a new type of drop window.

The new team was so successful that the company adopted the name 'Strachan & Brown'. Before long,

AEC had added its name to the list of approved bodybuilders, so that Strachan & Brown-bodied AECs could be found in Britain and all over the world. The company built not only buses and coaches but anything that ran on wheels, a tradition that it maintained right through to the end of its existence. For example, at one end of the range was the 'Abbey'

sports car coachwork, contrasting with 'Curtiss' racing horseboxes at the other.

The fortunes of the company took a sharp downturn in October 1928 with the departure of W E Brown. There is a story, probably apocryphal, that when he was asked where he was going, he replied 'Duple'. His questioner retorted: 'They will

never amount to anything with a name like that!' What really shook the company to the core, though, was the death of the founder himself in 1929. The family rallied round and formed, for the first time, a limited company, Strachans (Acton) Limited, with E Marshall Strachan (chairman) and J Reith Strachan (managing director).

Bournemouth Corporation no.43 (LJ 1607) was a Thornycroft BC with 32-seat Strachans body which entered service in 1930. Note that the concept of dual doors, famous on the Bournemouth trolleybuses, was already in place. The clerestory roof was an anachronism, never usual on buses and already out of date on trams. It did look rather splendid, though.
All photos from G Burrows collection

Top: *When Cleethorpes Urban District Council began bus operation in 1931, it could hardly be said that its vehicles were what were normally seen in municipal fleets. Strachans built two of these bodies, with contemporary luxury motor car appearance, on Gilford AS6 chassis. Numbered 5/7 (FW 2065/2231), they would have been used to tempt the better-off residents to use the new facilities.*

Above: *This Thornycroft BC chassis fitted with a Strachans H28/26R body is a Midland General vehicle, though it is in the livery of the associated Notts & Derby Traction Co, also a member of the Balfour Beatty group. RB 2594 was new in 1930, but was not numbered until 1932, when it became no.77.*

These developments could not have come at a worse time, since the world had moved into severe depression. Sales never recovered to their former level, and the company struggled to make a living for many years.

Restructured

One person who retained complete faith in the company all her life was the widow of J M Strachan. She acquired all the remaining shares in the company in addition to her own. In 1935 she married Sir William Noble, and restructured the company under the new name Strachans (Successors) Ltd. In 1961 she sold the company to the Giltspur Group, with the stipulation that the Strachans name be retained for at least ten years. The Giltspur Group was itself part of a large financial organisation, and under it came activities as diverse as nightclubs and industrial packaging.

Giltspur owned a former aircraft repair factory at Hamble, in south Hampshire. It had been used, among other things, for the repair of Spitfires during World War 2. Giltspur re-located the Strachans factory and key personnel to Hamble from the Acton works, which was then closed and sold. The company was then re-named for the last time as Strachans (Coachbuilders) Ltd.

One of the exhibits at the 1932 Scottish Motor Show in Glasgow was this Gilford Zeus with a Strachans H54R body. The Zeus was the Gilford model 163D, which meant 16ft 3in wheelbase double-decker, and it was hoped that it would capture some of the market then being swallowed up by Leyland. Had the Zeus been introduced sooner it may have stood a chance. It had a Tangye six-cylinder oil engine which, like the controversial Gilford lowheight vehicle, was also destined for obscurity. The Zeus was first registered in 1933 as WG 1619, this being the next number after a pair of Leyland Cubs bought that year by W Alexander, in whose fleet the Gilford is believed to have been demonstrated. It became no.723 in the Western SMT fleet when that company bought it in 1934. Western reduced the seating capacity to H24/24R and in common with its Gilford single-deckers fitted it with a Leyland 8.6-litre diesel engine, retaining it in its fleet in this form until withdrawal in 1944.

For a time the company prospered under Giltspur, and around 1970 a new factory was set up at Eastleigh to provide facilities to build the projected new Ford A series vans. Despite considerable investment by both Ford and Giltspur, the model was doomed to failure. Changing circumstances led the Giltspur Group to close or curtail many of its activities, and Strachans did not survive to see the end of 1974.

Above: *In 1935 Birmingham Corporation ordered a batch of Daimler COG5 single-deckers. The majority had bodies by MCCW, but 15 of them were built by Strachans, whose publicity at the time stated that the bodies were 'all metal'. A close study of photographs of both the MCCW and Strachans vehicles has failed to show any differences between the two makes other than the name badge. So it seems likely that the framework at least was supplied to Strachans by MCCW, for assembly and completion at Acton. Interestingly, the batch of ten Daimler chassis immediately preceding this order was also for single-deckers, this time for Newcastle Corporation. Now we know that of these, five bodies were by MCCW and the other five were by Northern Coachbuilders, all using MCCW metal framework. Here again, the finished vehicles were all identical.*

contracts, many of them very large with few orders for buses, though a number of coaches could always be found going through the factory. World War 2 gave the company plenty of variety in the types of work offered, and it was one of the companies chosen by the Ministry of Supply to build utility bus bodies on Guy Arab chassis. The vast majority of these were lowbridge, to an uncompromisingly square design.

Disaster

An initial postwar attempt to build all-metal double deckers was a disaster, though its composite bodies were usually satisfactory. From the late 1950s onwards Strachans re-established itself in the municipal sector and received some good orders for both single- and double-deck buses. Unfortunately they were often let down by sub-standard quality, though there were many exceptions to this situation. It also built up an extremely good relationship with the Ministry of Defence, building many hundreds of buses on Bedford SB and other chassis. These were to a rugged all-metal design that was later adapted for civilian sales.

An unusual vehicle built in the mid-1960s was the Saddler rail coach, for an entrepreneur of that name. He had hoped to interest British Rail in the concept of the railbus, but despite having one built to show them, nothing further was heard. The vehicle languished at a disused station at Whickham in Hampshire until it was destroyed by fire by vandals.

The biggest customer at the Hamble works was the Ford Motor Company, whose Transit van factory was only a few miles away in Southampton. Strachans had specially designed a parcel van body in co-operation with Ford to provide a large capacity-van suitable for large but lightweight loads. Several thousand of these were built.

Somewhat naturally thoughts turned to converting one of these into a small bus (the term 'minibus' had yet to be invented). Once the idea had been proved, a new design was created using the parcel van outline, but under the skin was a new framework, unlike later creations by other manufacturers. So the 'breadvan' bus was born.

To describe all the products or list all the customers would require a very large volume indeed. The company built buses for London General until 1931, then concentrated on commercial vehicle

Opposite below: *In 1936 the Daimler Co Ltd (as it was then) ordered a double-deck body from Strachans to be mounted on COG5 chassis no.9654 for use as a demonstrator. This photograph shows the all-metal framework of the body before it was completed, registered BUC 268 and painted in Northampton Corporation livery. It is known that at this time Strachans had a designer capable of producing all-metal bodywork and there is certainly no similarity in this structure to that of MCCW, so it must be concluded that this is the first Strachans 'all-metal' body. Northampton Corporation bought the bus from Daimler in August 1936 and numbered it 84. Daimler must have been pleased because apart from wartime allocations no other chassis make was purchased by Northampton until CVG6 production had ended. A major rebuild of the body took place in 1947, when Northampton Corporation produced a completely new composite lower-deck framework for it. This shows just how serious the shortage of bodies was at the time. The vehicle was finally withdrawn and scrapped in 1957.*

Above: *Aldershot & District was probably the best commercial customer for Strachans bodies. In 1936 ten of these bodies were built on Dennis Lancet II chassis (BOT 288-307). Fitted with 32 seats of generous proportions, these, combined with the smooth-running Dennis engines, ensured a quiet comfortable ride. Since Aldershot is an army garrison town it followed that the fortunes of A&D were bound up with the army, mainly by carrying soldiers on leave, but there were other aspects. Readers will have noted the size of the roof-mounted luggage carrier; these were known as 'band boxes' and were on all the buses in this batch. Several of the regiments based around Aldershot had their own bands and these vehicles were frequently hired by them to transport the musicians and their instruments to concerts.*

Below: *What proved to be the only Strachans trolleybus bodies were built in 1939 on AEC chassis for Southend-on-Sea Corporation, whose general manager, Harold Muscroft, had previously been at South Shields. Muscroft introduced the light blue livery to Southend on these buses in place of the former green. He also specified a body design that was very closely related to the Weymann trolleybuses supplied to South Shields. Strachans won the body contract on price and delivery with a design that resembled Weymann's in many respects. Due to the war, nos.124-9 (BHJ 194-9) were sadly neglected and they were in a very run-down condition when they were withdrawn at the closure of the Southend trolleybus system in 1954.*

Top: *The only Strachans bodies for the Sunderland District Omnibus Co were built to the BEF (British Electrical Federation) postwar single-deck design. They were also the only AEC Regals in that fleet. There were eight of them, new in 1948; the photograph shows no.196 (GUP 540) in SDO's navy (almost black) and white livery with fine gold lining and garter style fleetname surrounding a monogram. The long, narrow destination indicator was also a feature of the fleet, and no route numbers were shown. SDO had never previously bought BEF bodies, though its prewar Leyland Tigers carried Roe bodies that had many similar features. Subsequently SDO bought BEF bodies built by Brush and Roe, mounted on Leyland PD1, PD2 and PSU chassis.*

Above: *In 1950 the Ministry of Transport amended the PSV Construction & Use regulations to allow single-deck buses to be built 30ft long instead of the previous 27ft 6in maximum. On the day that the amended regulation came into force, five Leyland Comets built to the newly permitted length were delivered to Homeland Tours of Croydon. With Strachans 37-seat coach bodies, these were the first and only 30ft-long normal-control Leylands to enter service in the UK. This photograph was taken by flash outside the Acton works at one minute past midnight to celebrate the event.*

Above: *This amazing confection was built for Highland Transport and exhibited at the 1950 Commercial Motor Show. It is a Guy Arab III with lowbridge 57-seat body – complete with platform doors – and became no.72 (EST 392) in the Highland fleet. Highland Transport had taken four Strachans double-deck bodies on Guy Arab II in 1946 as well as 13 single-deck bodies on Arab III chassis between 1947 and 1951, and might well have continued to support the coachbuilder if Highland Omnibuses, part of the state-owned Scottish Omnibuses Group, had not been set up in 1952. Unlike other contemporary Strachans all-metal double-deck bodies, which proved troublesome, as Highland Omnibuses E72 this bus survived until 1970, passing then for further service on Orkney.*

Below: *In 1951, Aldershot & District was still buying Dennis Lancet chassis when Dennis announced its Dominant underfloor-engined bus. Naturally A&D took one of the prototypes and naturally it had a Strachans body with 41 seats (HOU 900). Both the coachbuilder and the operator were unsure about styling and layout on these new chassis. The Strachans body was an uncomfortable mix of old and new, with a rather sad-looking droop to the windscreen corners. The 'central' entrance was located just ahead of the rear axle, and just look at the odd back-to-front styling of the mudguards. Powered by a Dennis 06H engine, transmission was through a Hobbs automatic gearbox; this was soon replaced by a conventional Dennis gearbox. The photograph shows the bus before the Dennis nameplate had been fitted to the front. Only one other Dominant bus was completed; a third chassis was built but was dismantled without ever receiving a body.*

Reducing numbers

Full-sized buses continued to be built at Hamble, though in steadily reducing numbers. The last large orders were for Wolverhampton (the final double-deckers) and Sunderland corporations. There were lots of small orders by way of compensation, from private firms, local authorities and even a few for export. In 1967 Giltspur ordered Strachans to end PSV bodybuilding, but this order was never totally accepted.

For instance, many of the existing designs continued to attract orders from small operators, and the PSV-approved version of the Transit 16-seater was selling well. Not only that, but in 1966/7 the company put together a tender for the full production order of AEC Merlins for London Transport. If the company had been awarded this work, not only would it have survived longer but LT would also have been saved a lot of embarrassment, because alone amongst rear-engined single deckers, Strachans bodies proved to be problem-free.

Licence

In 1971 Strachans entered into an agreement with the Superior Coach Corporation of Lima, Ohio, USA. The Superior bodies were to be built under licence using a combination of Strachans and Superior components, all to Superior design. Similar agreements had previously been made between Superior and Plaxton and MCCW. One complete body and a batch of CKD (completely knocked-down) components were sent to Singapore, but the arrangement was allowed to lapse.

When Ford began the development work for its

Hall Bros operated a well-patronised express coach service between South Shields and Coventry for many years. In 1954 it bought six Leyland Tiger Cub chassis, which were fitted with 41-seat centre-entrance coach bodies. Two of them were by Harrington, the other four by Strachans as illustrated by CU 6952. The all-metal Everest design was of similar appearance in many respects to the Leyland coach body, but at an unladen weight of 6tons 4cwt it must have been a struggle for the small Tiger Cub engine to cope with a full load of passengers and luggage. All six were sold in 1959 and neither coachbuilder was favoured with Hall Bros orders again, but there were to be several more Tiger Cubs in the fleet.

projected A series van, it naturally turned to Strachans for the bodywork production. A factory was set up at Eastleigh, not far from the Ford works, with a production line similar to that at Hamble for the Transit. The A series did not live up to expectations, and the line never ran at full capacity, with production ending in 1974.

This was effectively the end for Strachans; Hants & Dorset took the Eastleigh works for use as its heavy repair works, and the Hamble factory was sold to Glover Webb, makers of heavy commercial vehicles. The Dormobile company bought the design rights for the Transit bus body, and production of these continued for some years at Folkestone.

Finally, a word about pronunciation. Strachan is a Scottish name pronounced with a soft 'ch' (as in 'loch') in the middle. The firm was based in London and the south of England, however, where the anglicised pronunciation 'Strawns' was always used by the company. So how you said it depended on where you lived!

Above: *The Ayrshire Bus Owners' Association (A1) was formed in 1926 to protect the interests of a number of small operators against the large companies. Their operations were based at Ardrossan on the coast of the Firth of Clyde. In 1963 the group bought four new double-deckers; three were AEC Regent V (WCS 194-6) and there was one Leyland PD2A/30 (WCS 197 shown here). They all had Strachans H35/28R bodies fitted with platform doors. The livery of the group was blue, with white window frames and a maroon flash above the lower deck windows. The 'route number' box in the photograph would be fitted with the 'A1' indicator before entering service.*

Below left: *Guy Motors (Europe) Ltd, as it was renamed after the take-over by Jaguar Motors, showed its prototype Arab V at the 1963 Scottish Motor Show. It appeared in the Kelvin Hall demonstration park, fitted with a new design of body by Strachans. The chassis was fairly conventional, with Gardner 6LW engine, fluid flywheel and semi-automatic gearbox, but was made lower than previous Arabs to allow a front-entrance body with reasonable step heights. The Strachans all-metal body featured the newly fashionable peaked domes and an almost square vertical rear end. There were 41 upper-deck seats and 31 downstairs, leaving little space for the staircase, which was consequently of a very tightly curved spiral shape. Wolverhampton Corporation was sufficiently impressed to place an order for 35, with the front and rear domes of a more conventional shape. Those features and a number of others were altered to match the details of simultaneous batches of Arab Vs entering service at Wolverhampton with Park Royal and MCCW bodies. The show bus was registered 888 DUK by Guy and was used as a demonstrator for the next three years, until Harper Bros. of Heath Hayes bought it in 1966.*

Above: *Whilst it did not receive the accolade of a 'by appointment' crest, London coach operator Charles Rickards was used very much by the 'upper crust' when attending functions for which convoys of cars would have been unsuitable. This was reflected in the discreet maroon livery with gold or silver trim & fleetnames. In 1964 it purchased six Dodge S307 coaches, three with 41-seat and three with 39-seat Strachans coach bodies. The front-mounted engine was the Perkins 6.354 and this was the largest order received for the model. AYV 96B shown here was one of the 39-seat versions with Strachans Pacesetter bodies, one of a range of 'Pace' bodies developed over the next few years. Rickards was taken over in 1968 by Frames Tours, which disposed of the Dodges.*

Below: *Designed for the Ford R192 chassis, the Strachans Pacesaver II body took to the roads in 1965. R I Davies, Tredegar, Monmouthshire, took delivery of no.55 (GAX 606C), this 45-seater in its red/cream livery. The design, with its double-curvature windscreens and rear glasses, was clearly aimed at BET companies though with limited success, because Marshall, Weymann and Willowbrook were already selling very similar bodies. The 'Pace' range of bodies sold well to the independent sector and was often used by councils for welfare and similar work.*

Top: *North Western nos.130-9 (AJA 130-9B) were surely the most unusual of the modern generation of Strachans single-deckers. Built in 1964 on Bedford VAL chassis, in itself an unfamiliar choice for bus work, they seated 52 passengers. The reason for the choice of chassis, and their claim to fame, was that with their low height and body design they could pass under a low arched bridge previously restricted to more conventional front-engined single-deckers. The arched roof style was last seen on a batch of Picktree-bodied AECs in the Northern General fleet in the 1950s, but it was a very common shape on buses of as far back at the 1920s.*

Above: *At first glance the Strachans bodies fitted to the AEC Swift chassis for Southampton Corporation in 1967/8 appeared to be the same as the London Transport XMS/XMB classes. There were, though, several major differences as seen on no.1 (JOW 499E), including shallower roof and windows, with moulded glassfibre front panel prominently featuring the AEC badge. Five similar 47-seaters followed, this time without the protruding side route number box, and with the lower edge of the skirt panels painted red. The Southampton buses featured the AEC type AH505 engine, of 8.19-litre capacity. Four more Swifts came in 1969, but their bodies were built by East Lancs.*

Above: *The Bedford VAS chassis provided the foundation for the extremely popular Strachans Pacerider body, suitable for 29 bus or coach seats. They were found in a variety of uses, as PSVs with small operators, welfare vehicles and even as long-distance coaches. Here is YMB 437F in the car park at the Hamble works, ready for despatch to a Bedford dealer. Such dealers often ordered batches of Pacerider for stock sales. Autotours of London placed regular orders for them. Fitted with luggage boots and roof racks, they toured the world with students and young people.*

Above: *When the agreement for the manufacture of the Superior body lapsed, Strachans designed a body using similar construction principles. The SC, as it was designated, could be modified to fit any of the current British bus or lorry chassis, either complete or CKD. Whilst they were not the prettiest vehicles ever built, their rugged simplicity won them many customers at home and abroad, but the only municipal order came from Bournemouth Corporation. The picture shows a Ford R226 with left-hand drive, the first of a batch for a Middle East oil producer; the remainder were delivered CKD. The raised, stiffened exterior waistrail served the same purpose as the similar feature which was a characteristic of Roe bodies.*

I would like to acknowledge the help and encouragement of the many people who have helped with this article, including Dave Griffiths, Robin Hood, David Hoy, Bill Wilson, and in particular former Chief Designer Jimmy Godden, who ensured that much of the archive material was saved from destruction. **CB**

No.3: Dennis Loline

Born: September 1956

Parents: Dennis Bros and Bristol Commercial Vehicles

Product of a long marriage or a one-night stand?: Perhaps more of a whirlwind affair and a touch of necessity. By the early 1950s, Dennis was neither the force it had been in the double-deck bus market nor was it the force it would become in much more recent times. Its Lance K4 was something of a 'me too' product in a market in which other people also built half-cab 'deckers with Gardner engines and crash gearboxes. Bristol used to build quite similar vehicles but was in the interesting position of having the revolutionary lowheight Lodekka in its range, but couldn't sell it to private sector companies.

Why not?: Because the rather rushed nationalisation of the Tilling Group's bus interests had left insufficient time to separate Bristol's manufacturing and operating activities. Motor manufacturers' lobbying ensured that Parliament wouldn't let any subsidiary of the British Transport Commission sell products on the open market.

So where did Dennis come in?: It desperately needed a more interesting product and had nothing like the Lodekka with which to try and tempt BTC fleets. A deal was struck for Dennis to build the Lodekka under licence and sell it to those parts not reached by the real thing. In essence, that meant BET companies, municipals, independents and export buyers.

Was it just the same as the Bristol?: Very similar, but not identical. In fact, the first vehicle – displayed at the Earls Court show in 1956 – was built from Bristol parts and, for all we know, might even have been a Bristol in disguise. The bonnet assembly was similar to that on the then current Lodekka LD, but Dennis took advantage of new legislation and offered it from the outset to the new 30ft length not yet available from Bristol. Bodywork also differed, for Eastern Coach Works was bound by the same restrictions as Bristol, so its Lodekka body couldn't go on the Dennis. Instead, these came from East Lancs, Willowbrook and Northern Counties. Then somebody wanted a different sort of Loline.

Who was that?: Edgley Cox, the strong-minded Walsall general manager who liked to buy buses like nobody else's. What he wanted from Dennis was tame by comparison with some of his requests. Just a forward-entrance version.

How was that done?: By creating the Loline II. This took a design from Bristol's drawing board (it would later emerge as the FSF/FLF Lodekka) and producing the first one in 1958, a couple of years before production versions of either the Dennis or Bristol version would appear. This also led to some variation beneath the bonnet.

And what was that?: While those same restrictions on BTC meant Dennis couldn't offer the Bristol engines available on the Lodekka, Dennis wasn't tied to offering the Gardner alternative, even if that was what most customers preferred. Dennis did make its own engines, but these weren't offered. Instead it plugged gaps and weaknesses in two of its larger rivals' ranges.

And you're going to tell us what they are: Leyland didn't yet have a lowheight version of its best-selling Titan PD2 or PD3, while AEC's integral Bridgemaster wasn't everybody's cup of tea. More like some people's cup of hemlock, truth be told.

So what did Dennis do?: It offered the Loline II with optional Leyland and AEC engines. Leyland versions went to Luton and Barton, AECs to City of Oxford.

This was the final version?: No. The Loline III, with revised gearbox and clutch (and the option of a semi-automatic gearbox) appeared from 1961 until production ended in 1967 with a small batch for Halifax. By then, Dennis was struggling to survive in almost any form and it seemed like the company had built its last bus. Happily, that turned out to be far from the case, but it was the end of the Loline.

How many were there?: There were 280, of which 141 went to BET's Aldershot & District – Dennis's local operator and also the last customer for the Lance K4 in 1954. The only others that took them into double figures were North Western (50), Reading (26) and Walsall (17). Hardly the volumes that make a wonderbus, but the engineering pedigree ensured it wasn't a blunderbus, either. Although there was one extremely unusual example.

Which was?: Barton 861, the lowest British double-decker in living memory. This Northern Counties-bodied 68-seater was just 12ft 5in high and was designed to fit under a bridge otherwise only capable of being negotiated by single-deckers. This was achieved by putting a lowbridge sunken gangway body on to a lowheight chassis – which must have meant only dwarfs could sit downstairs under the gangway. But it was a classic example of proving that something will be done if it can be done, even if no one ever tried to do it again.

Alan Millar

Two Aldershot & District Lolines compared – no.337 on the right is from the company's first, 1958 batch, with East Lancs rear-entrance body, and no.412 is a 1961 Loline III with forward-entrance Alexander body. They are seen at Aldershot in 1973.
Michael Dryhurst

LIKE THE
BACK-END
OF A BUS

Often an insult – and perhaps deservedly so when you see some buses – back-ends of buses are rarely photographed, causing problems for preservationists and modellers. Fortunately, CHRIS PALMER has been taking rear views

Portsmouth Corporation no.33, a 1949 all-Crossley DD42/7 in superb condition in spite of its imminent withdrawal, outside City Hall in 1967.
All photos by Chris Palmer

Above: *Eastbourne's old garage at Churchdale Road with (from left) 1946 Leyland PD1 no.15, 1951 AEC Regent III no.45 and 1966 Leyland PD2A/30 no.79, all theoretically with East Lancs bodies – though the AEC has Bruce bodywork on East Lancs frames.*

Below: *Southend Corporation no.330, a 1963 Albion Lowlander LR7 with Alexander forward entrance body, outside Southend Central station in 1968 after passing under the low bridge that caused the fleet to have gems such as this as well as AEC Bridgemasters and lowbridge Leyland Titans. The three-piece rear indicator is of interest.*

Above: *Chris Palmer suggests that this might be London's most handsome bus, a view that might not be universally shared – he suggests the affinity to Brighton AECs might affect his judgement. London Transport RLH50 of Addlestone garage leaves the old Onslow Street bus station in Guildford in 1968. The lack of a rear destination display is very non-LT.*

Below: *Displaying the famous Harrington dorsal fin, a Leyland Comet from the fleet of S M Tidy, the Brighton contractor and road haulier. It is seen in 1968.*

Above: *A newer Harrington dorsal fin body, a Wayfarer fitted to ex-Silver Star Leyland Tiger Cub OHR 281 of Wilts & Dorset, but on loan to Shamrock & Rambler and painted in S&R orange/ cream livery for the summer season in 1967.*

Below: *Reading Corporation 1961 Sunbeam F4A/Burlingham trolleybus no.184 at Tilehurst terminus, just as a snowstorm was starting, in 1968 about a month before the system closed. Some of these handsome buses earned a brief reprieve at Teesside, but others were scrapped.*

Above left: *Thames Valley no.H16, one of several Duple-bodied Guy Arab III inherited from Red & White's Newbury & District subsidiary. Dating from 1950, this is a highbridge example, seen at Newbury garage in 1968. A front view of a similar bus appears elsewhere in this book.*

Above: *The photographer's all-time favourite batch of buses were Southdown's 1955/6 Park Royal-bodied Guy Arab IVs. No.547, now preserved but seen in 1967, had this unusual inward-sliding door.*

Left: *Another Southdown Park Royal Guy Arab IV, this time with more typical four-leaf folding doors. No.530 is on the A23 road on the 117 Horsham-Brighton service in 1967. Like many operators, Southdown did not always use its rear indicators to full advantage.*

Above:
*Southdown
managed to
squeeze four
adverts around
the back of
no.335, a 1948
all-Leyland
PD2/1. It is seen
in Old Steine,
Brighton, on the
frequent 13 route
to Coldean Estate
in 1964.*

Left: *Southdown
no.761, a 1953
Northern
Counties-bodied
Leyland PD2/12,
in Midhurst High
Street at the end
of the long 22
route from
Brighton in 1967.*

Above: *Brighton Corporation 1947 AEC Regent III/Weymann no.86 of the undertaking's first postwar batch of Regents, at Old Steine on the former trolleybus route 26A to Preston Drove.*

Left: *The famous blue/cream AEC Renown/Park Royal demonstrator 7552 MX at Seaford in 1964 working for Southdown on the gruelling Brighton-Eastbourne 12 route. Southdown can't have been impressed, as it continued to favour Queen Mary Leyland PD3s.*

Above: *West Bridgford UDC no.32 seen just after crossing Trent Bridge from Nottingham in 1968 just weeks before the undertaking was absorbed into Nottingham City Transport. It is a 1957 AEC Regent V with Reading lowbridge body.*

Below: *Provincial (Gosport & Fareham) no.43, a new Seddon Pennine IV with Pennine bodywork, at Gosport Ferry in 1968.*

Above: *Back and front – Portsmouth Corporation's nos.5 and 6 at Southsea Common in 1968. They are 1935 Leyland TD4s with English Electric bodies. All four of this batch of open-toppers are now preserved.*

Below: *Classic Blackpool – centre-entrance Burlingham-bodied Leyland PD2/3s at Rigby Road garage in 1968. The beading below the rear emergency exit on these all-Lancashire buses – bodies built in Blackpool – shows where the third green band used to be.*

Above: *Chester Corporation no.78, a 1950 Foden PVD6 with Massey bodywork clearly showing the D-shaped lower-deck windows and the divided rear platform window.*

Below: *Brighton, Hove & District no.13, a 1960 ECW-bodied Bristol FS6B, seen in 1968. Most FSs had doors, so the lower-deck rear was completely different.*

LEAVING
LANCASHIRE

Respected transport journalist, JOHN ALDRIDGE, looks back at Lancashire in his last days as editor of *Leyland Journal*. John contributes the popular I Invited Myself feature in *Classic Bus* magazine

An exotic pair in Preston coach station, both on the X35 Skipton-Llandudno service. The route began in the early 1960s and was jointly licensed to Bracewell's (Colne), Crosville, Ribblesdale Coachways, Ribble and Standerwick. A Ribblesdale AEC Reliance/Yeates stands alongside a Ribble Leyland Leopard/Harrington.
All photos by John Aldridge

I HAD BEEN working and living in Lancashire for over five years when, out of the blue, came a job offer I couldn't refuse, but based back in London. Once the offer had been accepted and confirmed there came the realisation that there were many transport things that I had meant to look at and photograph, but had never got around to. Weekends were not necessarily going to be free before I actually moved, since there were more pressing matters such as selling the house and finding another, and calling on friends once more before moving.

All this was back in 1966, at a time when there

Left: *A brand-new Lancashire United Daimler Fleetline on the X60 Manchester-Blackpool service pauses at a hostelry for a refreshment stop. Note the shrouds round the engine covers on the Northern Counties body. All around are other buses on express workings.*

Below: *A North Western AEC Renown/Park Royal in Preston on the X60. It was new in 1963, the same year that the operator also bought a batch of Daimler Fleetlines.*

Passengers board and leave the ex-demonstrator Albion Lowlander of Bamber Bridge Motor Services in Preston's basic Starchhouse Square bus station . . .

were still numerous local authority-owned bus operators in Lancashire and when Ribble was still a bus operator of considerable size and standing. Indeed, the county of Lancashire as then constituted contained 27 of the country's municipalities. Not all the municipals were large and there was also still the odd, small independent, such as Bamber Bridge Motor Services, which ran into Preston from the town of its title. I can recall a very wet winter's morning soon after I moved into the area when I travelled on a Ribble bus into Preston from Chorley. We stopped by a somewhat inadequate queue shelter in Bamber Bridge under which a rather large number of people were attempting to shelter. All would have be travelling into Preston, my bus was going there, but few boarded it. They were waiting for the BBMS bus: local loyalty was strong.

I was lucky in that my move south would be toward the end of summer, so photographs could be taken in light evenings. Blackpool would be busy too. It was not as if I had not taken plenty of bus photos during my stay but the problem – if one can call it that – was the old one of having noted particular locations where the background was good or where the juxtaposition of vehicles could be of above average interest. One makes a mental note to go there again and spend an hour or so taking photos at some time in the future, but somehow never does. My bus photography has always been mainly a question of what appealed, rather than an urge to photograph, say, every batch of MCW Orion-bodied buses in a particular fleet.

But a move away also induces doubts. Has one really got a decent picture of a Rochdale Corporation

AEC Regent V in Manchester, where AECs were rare? And what about Wigan Corporation's rather mixed fleet of Leylands, where the body orders for each batch of chassis were often split between the two local bodybuilders, Northern Counties and Massey Bros?

X60

Then there was that remarkable express service, the X60, running from Manchester to Preston and Blackpool and which on summer weekends came up to a 15-minute timetabled frequency, with in addition much duplication or triplication or more. It boasted three resident operators in shared proportions: Ribble with seven-twelfths, North Western Road Car with three-twelfths and Lancashire United with two-twelfths, but with much hiring-in from other operators at busy times. Thus you had unlikely operators such as Leigh Corporation appearing on it, and indeed some of the hiring was so regular that several of the municipalities had its destinations and route number on their blinds. When I first arrived in the area I was amazed to see some of the buses turned out for it, such as North Western's prewar Bristol K5Gs with postwar Willowbrook lowbridge bodies. Imagine going for a 50-mile ride on one of those! Easter Monday was, I learnt, the busiest day of the year for the route, since the exodus from Blackpool from lunchtime onwards would have to handle not only returning day-trippers but also those who had spent the weekend

. . . while after takeover by Ribble in 1967 the Lowlander is seen in the attractive Lord Street, Southport, bus station that was originally a railway station.

in the resort. In 1964 from 11.30 onwards a total of 193 duplicate journeys were run on the Easter Monday with the peak peak time (in a manner of speaking) being between 18.30 and 19.00 when 25 double-deckers left Blackpool.

In the early days of rear-engined double-deckers there was considerable doubt among operators over new vehicle selection. LUT split some double-deck orders between Guy Arabs and Daimler Fleetlines, North Western dithered between AEC Renowns and Fleetlines while Ribble bought Leyland Atlanteans before reverting for a time to Leyland Titans. All could be found side by side on a good weekend, a particularly good location being a public house midway between Chorley and Preston on a Saturday morning, where buses, crews and passengers often took a break. The terminal at Manchester's Lower Moseley Street bus station (LMS on the destination blinds was not a reference to a former railway company) was a somewhat congested and chaotic place on a Saturday morning, though it did have the merit of some other services (express and stage) and their operators. An early evening line-up at the Blackpool end could be varied and impressive too, with vehicles on other express services from Yorkshire operators and others also loading.

In later years, after I moved, the advent of more motorways (Preston had had the first, even before the first section of the M1 opened) and what I can only assume must have been some kind of mental stagnation resulted in the Manchester-Blackpool

operation virtually fading away, though there was a motorway X61 for a time.

Surprise

A Sunday morning surprise, back in the early 1960s was again with the X60 when I saw a Trent AEC Regal, rebuilt to full front, in Chorley bus station. This was a working which I believe at one stage brought a complaint to the Traffic Commissioners and, subsequently, a reprimand, for the Trent workings were running into Manchester on a service from Derby, with the vehicles continuing to Blackpool on hire to Ribble on the X60. But they were leaving Derby with a Blackpool destination displayed, yet the company did not have a licence for such a service: Barton had that service. Subsequently, I think the Trent vehicles displayed a Manchester destination but with an additional windscreen sticker reading 'for Blackpool'. The opening of more motorways posed some problems for operators in that they offered far quicker journey times and thus better driver and vehicle utilisation, but at the expense of some intermediate traffic. However, before the advent of motorways, even a town like Chorley had some quite useful express services, such as the Manchester-Glasgow route,

Above: *Preston Corporation's services used street loading points in the town until 1969. An MCW-bodied Leyland Titan wears one of the experimental new blue/cream liveries tried out in 1966/7. Behind it is one of the corporation's 1952 Leyland-bodied Titans rebuilt in the transport department's workshops to 30ft long; it lasted until 1978.*

Below: *Fishwick's former Glasgow, former Leyland demonstration Atlantean is en route to Preston, turning by the then Royal Tiger-named public house.*

Above: *New building is evident in Manchester, but the PTE has yet to arrive as a Rochdale Corporation AEC Regent V/Weymann leaves for its home town.*

Below: *A dull day in Lancashire, but somebody is sweeping the pavement while a rare Accrington Corporation Guy Wulfrunian with rear-entrance East Lancs body lays over before leaving for Oswaldtwistle.*

operated jointly by Ribble and Western SMT, and Premier Travel's Blackpool-Clacton service. Early on a Friday evening in summer there were usually two vehicles on the inbound Manchester service, the first being a Western black-and-white-liveried Leyland Leopard with Alexander Y type coach body, while its duplicate was usually a cream and red Western dual-purpose Leopard with Y type body.

A problem in Chorley for the dedicated bus photographer was on a Saturday morning. The bus station would indeed see plenty of express service traffic, but some X60 duplicates, for example, would be fully loaded and keep to the main road, through the town, missing the bus station altogether. With vehicles passing on the main road (which would include those that had previously called at the bus station) one only got one chance for a photo, whereas the bus station doubled one's chances at least, as one could get the vehicle on its way in, stationary, or on the way out.

Preston presented a greater conundrum because in my time there were four bus stations. That of course was before one impressive new one was built in the late 1960s, eliminating all four. Now there are apparently doubts about the future of the present station.

But 35 or 36 years ago, well-known local independent John Fishwick & Sons had its own bus station in Fox Street, not far from the railway station, while Bamber Bridge Motor Services was using Starchhouse Square, once the home of several independent operators' services including Scout Motor Services, which was bought by Ribble in December 1961. Ribble and other express service operators used a relatively modern coach station,

which also served as terminal for a few Ribble stage services for which there was insufficient room in the main bus station nearby. And none of the stations were used by Preston Corporation, which exclusively used street termini for all its local services. These were generally distinguished from one another not by route numbers but by route letters, so that for example Corporation buses to Moor Nook were route MN while those to Farringdon Park were FP.

Prosperous

A favourite place to visit in those days was Southport, perhaps then a rather more prosperous resort than it is today. Then it also had its own smartly painted and maintained and well-run municipal fleet, with one Roy Marshall (well-known to *Classic Bus* and *Classic Bus Yearbook* readers) as traffic superintendent. But it was not until a visit to the town in the early 1970s and a ride on one of the Corporation's former Ribble PS2 Leyland/ Burlinghams converted to open-top that I realised that much of the town had been laid out in American style on the grid system.

Roy Marshall was then also one of my most useful contacts with information and help for articles on the bus side of *Leyland Journal*. One interesting trial carried out in Southport in 1965 used a hired Manchester Corporation rear-engined Leyland Panther on a one-bus local route on which a flat fare of 3d (2d for children) was experimentally charged.

Top: *A Leyland Leopard of Western SMT with Alexander Y type coach body is in Chorley en route for Glasgow with its crew of two.*

Above: *By the time this picture was taken the previously independent Scout Motor Services had become a subsidiary of Ribble. Scout's no.S4, a former Ribble Atlantean, is on the X60 in Chorley and correctly carries an 'On Hire to Ribble' label in its front nearside windscreen.*

Outside the busy Preston coach station stand a Ribble White Lady Atlantean dating from 1962 on a Blackpool service and a Standerwick Gay Hostess Atlantean of 1960 on the London service.

Passengers paying with a 3d piece boarded on the right-hand side and used a self-service ticket machine while other adults and children boarded on the left and paid the driver. The machine was a version of one used in Copenhagen, Denmark, but Southport was the first UK user. The idea was to try to speed up fare collection on one-man operated buses, a matter that still occupies many minds today.

Towns

One of the delights of Lancashire was – and still is – the way you can often turn a corner in a town and find yourself suddenly in attractive open country. But for the bus enthusiast it was of course the towns and their PSV content that were of the greatest interest. Bolton Corporation was probably the most interesting local operator, with its attempts to give buses a better image, culminating in its striking fleet of Leyland Atlanteans. But there were others who were working hard to provide more attractive interiors, such as Harry Taylor, then general manager at Oldham Corporation. With all the talk there has always been about road-rail integration it always surprised me that Manchester's Piccadilly station (previously named London Road) had only one bus route terminating there, that being for many years an Oldham one. But then when I look at today's main Piccadilly bus station with its miserable queue shelters and numerous services banished elsewhere I can only conclude that bus passengers are worse off than they were in my day. Then too the much busier Victoria and Exchange stations (only Victoria

survives) also had a convenient if basic and cramped bus station adjacent, and actually in Salford.

Blackburn is another Lancashire town that boasted its own municipal fleet – and still does (albeit at arm's length), and was another operator with an interesting fleet, perhaps because of all those Guy Arabs. The oldest dated from 1949 and had Crossley bodies (which, unlike the firm's engines, had an excellent reputation).

But it was slightly further afield, to Accrington, that I was particularly attracted. That was not for its town centre or market but because of the unusual dark blue and red livery, which was quite unlike almost any other livery found on a municipal bus. There were also its two 'mistakes' — the unique Guy Wulfrunians, not with the front entrances which this front-engined bus was designed for, but with rear-entrance East Lancs bodies, and seats for only 68. Near Accrington, at Oswaldtwistle, was the terminus of a very strange route, developed and operated by Ribble. The Oswaldtwistle-Southport service ran every two hours and was to me the most bizarre result of a bee-in-the-bonnet of Ribble's general manager, Horace Bottomley. He saw the economic merit of linking two or more routes into one long one. New journey opportunities would be created and running costs would be lowered because long

Above: *A Trent Alexander-bodied Leyland Tiger Cub semi-coach leaves Preston bus station for Blackpool with blinds set for the X60, having earlier worked into Manchester on another service. The sticker in the nearside windscreen is a left-over from the earlier run and reads 'for Blackpool' but the vehicle is not carrying any 'on hire' label.*

Below: *Ribble had rural territory too, including of course much of the Lake District. Many of its first Leyland underfloor-engined buses, the integral Leyland-MCW Olympics, were based here.*

routes needed shorter lay-over times than would previously have been needed in total by their constituent parts.

While one could see the sense of the idea in, say, the Blackpool-Preston-Blackburn-Rochdale route, it seemed highly unlikely that the 298's Oswaldtwistle-Blackburn-Leyland-Southport run created any new business. With a running time of 2hr 20min I doubt that many Oswaldtwistle or Blackburn folk made a day trip to Southport on it.

Wigan

Moving in the other direction, south of Chorley, was Wigan, then — as already mentioned – with its municipal fleet, but also well served by the large independent, Lancashire United, and by another municipality, Leigh Corporation. In the past Leigh had had unusual taste in bodywork, with Titans and Regents with Roberts bodies and other Titans with Lydney bodies. East Lancs had become the preferred bodybuilder for some years, with latterly, lowheight bodies on Dennis Lolines and AEC Renowns, with one batch of Renowns unusually having rear-entrance bodies. But the reason for the all lowheight double-deck fleet was not a low bridge in an awkward place but a low garage roof.

One of the delights of the north west in the 1960s was the operation of so many longer-distance routes and also some joint routes, so that municipal buses could often be found on bus routes somewhat away from their home base.

Thus, for example, one could find St Helens Corporation buses in Southport, though not the opposite: Southport Corporation buses did not run to St Helens. In my time a regular performer on the Southport service was its one and only 30ft-long double-decker, and also its only forward-entrance double-decker, a 1959 East Lancs-bodied AEC Regent V.

Better-known St Helens buses were its London-style RT types with Park Royal bodies, of which no fewer than 40 had been bought primarily because of their relatively low height of 14ft 3^{1}/2in.

By no means all Lancashire or north-western bus operation was, or is, urban, and indeed Ribble's 298 service mentioned earlier was certainly a fairly rural route for much of its length. Then Ribble itself ran right up to the Lake District, then, less of a tourist honey-pot than today, when services are operated by successor Stagecoach Cumberland or Stagecoach in Cumbria – the county boundary was moved some years ago when Greater Manchester was created, and many other boundaries were changed. But there always have been tourists in the Lake District, and low-revenue bus routes too. Much of Ribble's operation in my time in that area was with its integral Leyland-MCW Olympics, though there were newer buses and coaches as well. A particular delight was the garage at Ambleside, opened in 1931 and demolished at the end of the 1980s. It was built in local stone, and blended nicely with the landscape.

North of the Lake District one came across a slightly different Ribble, with a fair number of double-deckers on busy city services in Carlisle. Variety then was the great feature of buses in the north west and usually the colour of the buses (or some of them) could tell you where you were: it was all far removed from the corporate colours of today. I only wish I had taken even more photos than I did, but that is a regret shared with many enthusiasts! **CB**

DOES NOBODY WANT ME FOR A SUNBEAM?

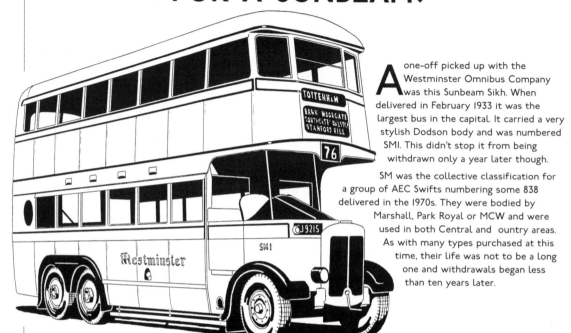

A one-off picked up with the Westminster Omnibus Company was this Sunbeam Sikh. When delivered in February 1933 it was the largest bus in the capital. It carried a very stylish Dodson body and was numbered SM1. This didn't stop it from being withdrawn only a year later though.

SM was the collective classification for a group of AEC Swifts numbering some 838 delivered in the 1970s. They were bodied by Marshall, Park Royal or MCW and were used in both Central and ountry areas. As with many types purchased at this time, their life was not to be a long one and withdrawals began less than ten years later.

GB's ABC
OF CB

Now that *Classic Bus* magazine is in its tenth year, editor GAVIN BOOTH takes an alphabetical look back at CB since 1992

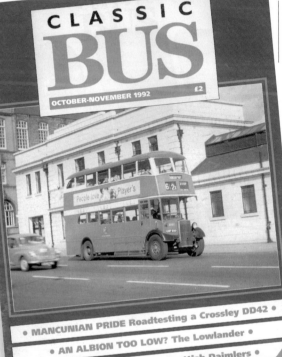

CLASSIC

BUS

OCTOBER-NOVEMBER 1992 £2

People love Player's

• MANCUNIAN PRIDE Roadtesting a Crossley DD42 •

• AN ALBION TOO LOW? The Lowlander •

• CANNY BUYS Postwar Scottish Daimlers •

FREE INSIDE
1952 RT ADVERT
Full-colour
Ready-to-frame
print

9 770966 843003

B is for Blunderbus. Right from issue no.1 Classic Blunderbus has been a popular and controversial page in every CB. It grew out of an article Alan Millar had written for *Buses Yearbook 1989* and Alan thought it could make a series. It did. Now roundly 60 issues later he is still finding bus and coach models that deserve the Blunderbus tag. Alan has, I know, a Blunder list, and he cleverly keeps some of his powder deliberately dry for later Blunderbi – so it took 56 issues to get to CIE's amazing but ill-fated Bombardiers, for instance *(see page 112)*. The Blunderbus page upsets readers when it features models close to their hearts and we get letters of protest. But, as Alan frequently points out, applying the definition doesn't imply a *bad* bus. Some were undoubtedly good but failed for other reasons – like the Leyland Titan TN15. Equally, some failed because they really *were* that bad – like the Daimler Roadliner.

C is for Crossley. Way back in issue 1 Stephen Morris roadtested preserved Manchester Crossley DD42/8S no.2150. Although Crossley was never in the same sales league as AEC or Leyland, it turned out that there were large numbers of closet Crossley fans among CB readers and Stephen unwittingly provoked a lengthy correspondence about the merits of the make. Now a definitive history of Crossley is well down the pipeline so the fans will have an opportunity to indulge their passion.

A is for Antecedents. CB's were pretty impressive: *Buses* and *Buses Extra*. The monthly *Buses* had spawned a bi-monthly offshoot, *Buses Extra*, and when publisher Ian Allan offered this title on a franchise basis Classic Bus Publishing Ltd was formed to take it on with a view to relaunching it as *Classic Bus*. So in September 1992 the now much sought-after issue no.1 *(above)* hit the bookstalls. CB was probably more focussed than BX; we had decided to aim firmly for the nostalgia market – for readers just like us, I suppose – and our audience seemed to appreciate that. Was it really 10 years ago? It seems like 20.

D is for Diecasts. There was a time, not long ago, when collectors of diecast buses had very little to spend their money on. After the collapse of Dinky Toys, Corgi picked up that mantle and produced toy buses, notably a Routemaster casting, while Solido offered its RT and Paris Renault models. As models they were okay, but they were largely aimed at the toy market and were out of scale for railway modellers. Then Corgi introduced a passable Duple A type halfcab coach on AEC Regal 'chassis' and it seemed that the chunky 1:50 scale was what we collectors could expect. Builders specialising in house extensions rubbed their hands in anticipation. It took Frank

Joyce to see the scope for 1:76 (00) scale models; Exclusive First Editions (EFE) was born and its first model, a London Transport RT, introduced us to a new level of accuracy and detail that appealed to collectors and kick-started the recent boom in bus diecasts. Corgi followed suit with its 1:76 scale Original Omnibus Company (OOC) range, and now the collector has up to a dozen new models every month to choose from, based on a growing range of castings of vintage and current models. Occasionally, both companies choose to model the same bus, as happened in 1995 with the MCW Orion body. The photo on the facing page shows EFE's Sheffield Regent V and OOC's Titan PD2.

CB's involvement? We have reviewed them since our early days and find ourselves consulted by EFE and OOC on vehicle types and liveries – all very even-handedly, of course. We ran a readers' poll to establish the Most Desirable Diecasts – the models they most wanted to see in model form – and while we would never assume that those nice folks in E17 and LE3 would be influenced by what our readers think, it is perhaps more than a coincidence that five of the top ten are now being produced or are promised – including the top four: the Bristol Lodekka, MCW Metrobus, Leyland TD1 and Leyland PD3 Queen Mary.

 is for Entertainment. CB has never really had a mission statement as such, but if we had one we could summarise it as 'to inform and entertain'. Yes, the information is important to readers, but we strongly believe that it must be tempered with enough lighter touches to keep readers entertained. For all of us, even those who make a living from our hobby, there has to be an element of enjoyment somewhere along the line. Hence the more informal writing style of some of our contributors balances the more erudite writings of others. Which is not to say that we don't take the magazine seriously. We do, but not *too* seriously.

 is for Fools, the April variety. A natural follow-on from the last item, perhaps. Like so many publications we have perpetrated the occasional April Fool on our readers. Some were blatant – 1994's Leyland Herculean *(right)* springs to mind – others more subtle – 2001's Frank

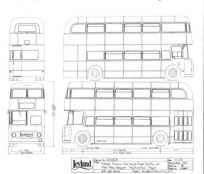

Pick/R Stuart Pilcher exchange of correspondence. Sometimes we don't include an April Fool and get letters from readers who have read the magazine from cover to cover and couldn't find it. Occasionally a genuine item is wrongly accused – the 1998 piece on Albion double-deckers operating in the Belgian Vicinal fleet, for example.

Most readers seem to enjoy them. Some accuse us of confusing future historians and insist on a statement in the next issue putting the record straight. Ho hum.

 is for Geoffs. At an early stage in CB's history it seemed that every other correspondent or contributor was called Geoff. Not true, of course, but in our 1996 April Fool we featured 'The Book of Geoffs' and the notion was born that the collective description 'Geoffs' could be applied to our knowledgeable, if occasionally controversial, contributors. Notable Geoffs hail from Hampshire, Surrey and Yorkshire, and in their defence they have all provided ready assistance and encouragement to your editor over the years.

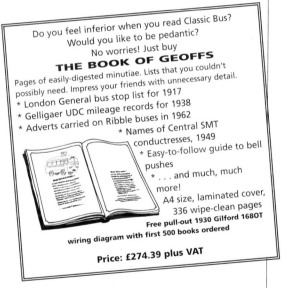

is for Head-to-Head. As in Tests, apparently a popular CB feature. Aided and abetted by Stephen Morris, your editor has been let loose on many prized and tasty vehicles in an effort to carry out the kind of comparison tests that the car mags do so well. We aim for like-for-like comparisons, not always practical, and started in a small way in 1994 with the London RT and its Leyland equivalent, the RTL. (Result: divided, with the RT favoured for intense urban work and the RTL for suburban and country work). Then we managed a three-way test in

1996 involving lowheight double-deckers – the AEC Renown, Bristol FLF and Dennis Loline. (Result: Loline popular, followed by FLF). In 1998 we tackled an AEC Reliance and Leyland Tiger Cub – each chassis had its pros and cons. In 1999 those kind people at Sandtoft let us loose on seven trolleybuses, not so much a head-to-head but great fun for two trolleybus-driving virgins. Meanwhile Steve Morris down in Somerset arranged a five-way test involving single-deckers of a certain age — AEC Regal, Bristol L5G, Daimler CVD6, Dennis Lancet J3, and Leyland Tiger PS1. With two buses to test it's likely we'll disagree; with five buses it's a racing certainty. The kindest way to sum this test up is to say that they all had their good points . . .

Since then we have tested three 30ft long rear-entrance double-deckers, an AEC Regent V, Leyland Titan PD3 and a Guy Arab IV. Here there was a fair degree of unanimity; unexpectedly, we loved the Guy, liked the AEC and hated the Leyland. There was total unanimity in our latest head-to-head, in 2001. We took a Leyland Titan TN15 and an MCW Metrobus from the White Rose fleet at Egham (with permission, of course) and drove these two former London buses, largely designed for London conditions – and fell in love with the Titan. The Metrobus was good, but the Titan – superb. Stephen said it was the best bus he had ever driven; praise indeed.

CLASSIC BUS

No51 FEBRUARY – MARCH 2001 £3.10

ROUTEMASTERS
The Northern
General version

MUNICIPALS
Edinburgh Guys
Bolton Leylands

MEMORIES
Jersey in colour
Montevideo's treasure

FAVOURITES
All our regular
columnists

RED ALERT
WE TEST THREE 30ft BACK-LOADERS

REMEMBERING BUSES THE WAY THEY USED TO BE

the boom in bus books over the past 30 years you might think that everything that everybody could possibly want to know about buses is already in print. Our experience is that there are a large number of enthusiasts whose lifetime studies into a particular aspect of our hobby will add to our combined knowledge and so we are happy to publish what may seem like highly-specialised articles. From the start we avoided the topics that have been or could be best covered in a book. A multi-part complete history of, say, AEC, is not for CB, but we are happy to share the history of the STL, or the story of Kent's Coaches of Baughurst.

is for Jowitt. Robert E of that ilk. Robert's, er, distinctive writing and photographic style have featured in the magazine and in the Yearbooks. He seems to infuriate and delight in almost equal measures with his off-beat photos – often involving attractive young ladies, it must be said – and brings a breath of fresh air to bus writing. I first came across his work when I was working as a book editor at Ian Allan, and oversaw production of his title *A Silence of Trolleybuses*. But it was many years before I met him. I was at a Fotobus meeting in Manchester and a group of us were standing in Piccadilly photographing the variety of buses that poured into the stops there. Then we noticed this sober-suited man photographing those same buses, but from further away. While we had picked our spot to avoid passers-by getting into shot, he had picked his to include them.

is for Kingdom, as in United. It's the area we major on – but see under S and X.

is for Information. The other part of our non-existent mission statement (see E). CB readers have an apparently insatiable appetite for information. With

 is for London. Not unrelated to the previous letter of the alphabet, London's transport history has a huge following. Look at the membership of societies like LOTS, and the wealth of London publications. Obviously a publisher, especially a Scottish-based one, can't afford to ignore London. Few of us, even in the 'provinces', would pretend that London's bus history is of no interest to us. To enthusiasts of A Certain Age, like your editor, there was little published material on non-London subjects available in the 1950s so we became London enthusiasts by default. Even though in the UK there are many, many times more people living outside London, CB recognises the need for a regular London 'fix'.

 is for Museums. The growth of the bus preservation movement was well advanced when CB was launched but we have been happy to acknowledge and support the work done in this area. We are happy to leave the nitty-gritty of preservation to other publications and with a bi-monthly publication, rally coverage is not for us. But we have been happy to support museums and events with sponsorship, recognising that they are an important part of preserving our transport heritage. And we happily acknowledge that certain museums and groups – they know who they are – have given CB immense help over the years.

 is for National, as in Leyland. A Classic Bus?, I hear you ask. We think so. Like it or not, the National sold in vast numbers and dominated the UK single-deck scene for a decade. Which leads to the question – how do you define a Classic Bus in terms of CB coverage? We have a rolling 20-year rule, so Nationals are in by a full decade, and models like the Metrobus and Titan, still seen on our streets, just squeeze in at the start of the 1980s. Not only that, but your editor's local operator, Lothian Buses, is actually introducing National 1s for the first time as it gathers secondhand Volvo-engined examples from all over Britain – and it's placing them into service alongside brand-new 51-registered Dennis Tridents (*above*). Quite a contrast.

 is for Open Platform. We wanted a back-page feature along the lines of the 'Day in the Life' articles in the weekend supplements, so Open Platform was born as a soapbox for CB readers to sound off on matters that bothered them. We started with a couple of commissioned pieces, then, as we had hoped, the readers rose to the challenge. We had readers sounding off on subjects as diverse as cherished registrations, problems for enthusiasts with disabilities, and the end of Green Line. John Aldridge leapt to the defence of the Leyland Panther after it had been Blunderbussed and Brian Dyes set the cat among the pigeons by suggesting that 9 out of every 10 preserved buses could end up scrapped.

More recently we found we were running out of contributions so Open Platform took a rest. Maybe readers had all got it off their chests – but knowing bus enthusiasts I very much doubt it. Maybe it will make a reappearance on page 54. It's up to you.

 is for Photography. Magazines like CB rely on a supply of good photos and fortunately for us there were plenty of you out there with your Box Brownie, Kodak Retinette and Ilford Sportsman cameras in the 1950s and 1960s to ensure a regular supply. Prewar photos can sometimes present a problem but we are fortunate that we can call on several notable photographers and collectors. The big excitement is when someone writes to us along these lines: 'I took these colour photos in the 1950s. Would you like to see them?' It happens. Even now there are roving bands of bus photographers (below) 'laying down' photos for CB in 20 years time.

 **is for Q&A.** What started as a bright idea from Geoff Burrows quickly grew into a popular and much-used feature. Readers provide questions asking about an amazing range of topics and Geoff burrows away ferreting out the answers. He readily admits that he isn't omniscient, but he certainly knows how to get hold of the info through a network of experts. His answers have covered everything from wheel-chocks to the vehicles used in the TV series *On the Buses*.

is for Roger. Roger as in Roger and Out – and indeed our Regular features. Magazines need regular features and editors need writers who can provide authoritative and entertaining copy for every issue –

on time. *Buses* magazine editor Alan Millar supplies Classic Blunderbus, as we have seen, and Checkpoint, a bi-monthly potted biography of some aspect of older buses. John Aldridge has provided some fascinating memories from his career in transport journalism in I Was There and now provides stories from his career under the title I Invited Myself. Former bus company manager Roger Davies joined CB at issue 50 with his Roger and Out tailpieces, reminiscing about his transport career in a distinctive and witty style. Other occasional features have included Type Approval, looking in detail at a particular bus, and Chassis Code Cracking, an attempt to decode the often complex designations adopted by manufacturers. Our most recent feature is Letters from London, where Chris Drew illustrates the very different London types that have shared the same type codes.

 is for Scottish content. Despite the fact that the editor (and indeed two of his fellow CB directors) are Scots, coverage of Scotland in CB is possibly proportionately poorer than coverage of other parts of the UK. The reason could well be that your editor bends over backwards to avoid any criticism that Scotland gets more than its fair share of CB column inches or – and this is true – contributors hold back submitting Scottish material, knowing the editor's background. The simple answer to this is – don't hold back, chaps.

 is for Trolleybuses. But probably not Trams. Trolleybuses obviously fall into the CB remit and we include trolleybus contributions whenever possible. Your editor, raised in a trolleybus-free environment, needed some convincing about their merits, but when those friendly folks at Sandtoft arranged the trolleybus head-to-head test, he was convinced. As a closet tram enthusiast I'd love to include more on those creatures that move in predestinate grooves, but dyed-in-the-wool busfans might not agree.

is for Update. The Classic Update pages are the nearest we get to topicality in CB. As the mag developed we appeared on more mailing lists and are happy to publicise events, restorations, merchandise – anything that seems to be of interest to old bus enthusiasts (that's enthusiasts of old buses, of

TROLLEYHEAD TO TROLLEYHEAD

STEPHEN MORRIS and **GAVIN BOOTH** jumped at the chance to drive trolleybuses at Sandtoft. Neither had ever driven a trolleybus, but they both had licences to drive motorbuses, and surely they couldn't be that different . . . Stephen takes up the story

Top: Lined up at Sandtoft, ready for SM and GB – Nottingham no.506, Rotherham no.631, Derby no.172 and Reading no.113. Photos by Gavin Booth

Below: Reading no.113, the 1939 Park Royal-bodied AEC 661T/Park Royal. 'It's a beautifully refined old lady, just like a 1939 Regent but without the noise. . . It has all the ambience and refinement of a very expensive luxury motorcar, both to drive and to ride in'.

TROLLEYBUSES were designed so that former tram dri~~ver~~ ~~eas~~ier to drive than ~~...~~

---

course). What sometimes surprises us is that we have never heard from some major societies and museums, so we can't feature their news.

is for Vintage, perhaps Veteran. My dictionary defines a veteran car as one built before 1905. It also defines a vintage car as 'an old motor car, specifically one built between 1919 and 1930'. What you call a car built between 1906 and 1918, I'm not sure, but while I'm happy to go along with the veteran definition, I take a broader view of 'vintage'. The term 'post-vintage thoroughbred' may be okay for newer cars. But buses?

is for Write to Reply. We didn't plan a letters page in CB. It just happened. After a few issues we started receiving letters with corrections and comments on CB items. There is no pattern. Some items that I think will produce an avalanche of mail don't. Others that seem very innocuous and unprovocative manage to

provoke – sometimes to the extent of several pages of closely-set A4. Needless to say, correspondents who are more economical with their words stand a better chance of getting into print.

is for Xenophobia. Not all CB readers, it must be said, have an interest that extends beyond these shores – some have problems beyond the M25. But easier and cheaper foreign travel means that many readers have an interest in the buses that can be found overseas. We usually resist the temptation to include material about older buses built outside the UK, but we know there is a growing interest in UK-built buses in other countries, either those exported when new or those sold abroad in recent years, often for painting in London-style red to masquerade as 'real' London buses. But you must admit that this CCFL, Lisbon, AEC Regent *(see page 118)* is a choice specimen.

 is for Yearbook. Indeed, what you are reading. Following in the footsteps of the popular *Buses Yearbook*, publishers Ian Allan thought there could be a market for a CB equivalent. This is no.8, so they must have been right. The Yearbook is just one of CB's spin-offs; we've done sweatshirts, mugs, calendars and special diecast models too.

 is for Zoo, the Leyland one. Well, what else could we include for Z? Bus enthusiasts very often have their favourite types. AECs and Bristols, for instance, each have a dedicated following. And your editor has regularly confessed to a weakness for Leylands, now nurtured by the Leyland Society (free plug). And the Zoo bit? Leyland's famous fondness for naming its models after animals – hence the Cheetah, Leopard, Lynx, Tiger, Royal Tiger, Tiger Cub (indeed Royal Tiger Cub) and Titan. Oh no, the Titan's not an animal, is it – unless you count the steering on a PD2.

No.4: Plaxton

CHECK POINT

Founded: Scarborough, 1907, by Frederick William Plaxton

To build coaches?: No. As a joiner, who subsequently branched out into plumbing and building contracting. Then World War 1 broke out and he got into munitions manufacturing. From that, he got into car bodybuilding and in an age when many coaches were really just scaled up large cars, and that led to diversification into charabanc building. By the end of the 1920s, Mr Plaxton dropped car bodying to concentrate on bodying buses and coaches.

Who bought them?: In the early years, they went mostly to Yorkshire operators, so it took time for them to be found elsewhere, but the opening of a new factory in 1936 prompted an increase in production and the establishment of links with dealers. These keys to Plaxton products reaching a wider market were London-based Arlington and Manchester's Lancashire Motor Traders. Most of these early bodies were on Bedford, Dodge, Leyland and AEC chassis, but there was also some valuable business to be won from operators seeking new bodies for older chassis. It wasn't yet in the same league as Duple, which enjoyed the fruits of a close marketing relationship with Bedford, but it was on the way up. Then war intervened.

What happened then?: It was plunged back into munitions manufacturing, whereas Duple was one of the favoured utility bus bodybuilders and gained as a result. Plaxton had to start all over again when hostilities ended.

What did it build?: Lots more of the sorts of coaches it had built in the late-1930s, except in greater numbers as there was an artificial boom in coach travel while petrol was in short supply for private motoring. As the boom subsided, the company diversified into some other things, notably bodying over 400 Bedford S-type Green Goddess fire tenders. It had a couple of other challenges to face.

And these were?: The slump in demand for new vehicles and the almost overnight replacement of half-cabs with underfloor-engined chassis at the heavy-duty end of the market. Projects like the Green Goddesses and later the introduction of bus bodies helped cushion the blow of the first of these, while rapid development of modern yet restrained body designs for the new generation chassis helped win business from important long-term customers like Wallace Arnold.

Why was restraint so significant?: Because some of the early, smaller builders of underfloor-engined coaches – to whit, Bellhouse-Hartwell and Windover, among others – produce some highly ostentatious designs that never caught on and dated almost overnight. Even Duple's Roadmaster did better as a Dinky toy than it ever did as a real working full-size coach.

How conservative were the Plaxton designs?: Not too conservative. And in 1958 BET's Sheffield United Tours subsidiary prompted Plaxton to develop one of the trendsetters of the late-20th century – the Panorama. This took advantage of emerging glass technology to have much longer windows, which provided touring passengers with better views outside. The success of the Panorama helped encourage the company to move to a larger new factory in 1961.

How did the Panorama evolve?: The general concept was adapted as styling fashions also encouraged the company to develop new styles of front and back ends. It also got longer, with the launch of new chassis following the legalisation of 36ft (11m) in 1961 and the subsequent adoption of 12m as the maximum length in the late-1960s. By then, the Panorama moved on to its final, great stage.

That was?: To become the Panorama Elite in 1968, with curved sides and round-profile windows. This model's launch coincided with and probably accelerated Duple's decline from glory. Plaxton soon established itself as market leader with coaches more in tune with what the market wanted. Indeed, four years later Duple was forced to fight back with its Dominant – designed by the man Duple managed to poach from Plaxton and with a highly familiar profile to anyone who knew what came out of Scarborough.

What did Plaxton do next?: It copied Duple's technology. Its rival's one remaining lead was to have adopted steel rather than timber framing, and Plaxton began doing this as it phased out the Elite from 1974 and replaced it with its similar but all-new Supreme. It evolved until its replacement by the Paramount range in 1982. By then, Plaxton was bodying a wide range of imported chassis it had never touched before, while the volumes of Bedford and Ford lightweights were plunging by the year. The company also went through a series of changes of ownership.

And what were these?: The coachbuilding side of the business was bought by the Kirkby Central dealer chain in 1987 and went on to acquire the wreckage of Duple in 1989. Around the same time, Plaxton also acquired the Henlys car dealer chain, but this business was actually larger than Plaxton and ended up effectively taking over Plaxton. Henlys later sold its car dealerships and merged Plaxton with Mayflower to create TransBus International, but that's all very recent history.

Alan Millar

Plaxton introduced this frontal style on its Consort body in 1956. This is an AEC Reliance with centre-entrance Consort body from the fleet of Valliant of Ealing.
Michael Dryhurst

GOOD STUFF

In the years 1930-3 many independents were taken over by the LGOC, introducing many weird and wonderful vehicles to the fleet. One such company was Charles Pickup, which operated the 37 group of routes that ran from one side of south London to the other. Apart from the famous open-top Regents, later to become STL553-7, this battle-tank of a Guy FXC was dumped on LGOC. This, along with similar vehicles from other firms, was put into the GS class.

In the early 1950s, the fleet of Leyland Cubs that had given sterling service were beginning to feel their age, so a joint specification was drawn up with Guy Motors to produce a 26-seat bus to replace them. The outcome was the Guy Special, a cross between the Vixen and Otter chassis and bodied by ECW. They were lettered GS and worked country routes on which it was not economic to operate larger buses. They did just manage to last into London Country ownership, with three used as staff buses making it to 1973. Have no fear, though, about never seeing another one, because there seem to be more in preservation than ever ran along the roads of the Home Counties.

ROGER AND OUT

Withdrawn busman ROGER DAVIES looks back at his first forays oop north

Only a Northern song

THERE MAY BE trouble ahead. The look on his face and the wagging finger told me Davies Senior was not best pleased with his offspring. I had a splendid reason for being two hours late home from school, so no worries there.

Had I not been waiting for the Fairwater to Victoria Park bus as usual when along came a yellow/cream Alexander-bodied Atlantean registered SGD 669? Had not even philistine non-bus enthusiast chums been impressed with this futuristic beast? And my knowledgeable account of it and the fact that it was from Glasgow, hence GCT on the staircase mirror and the distinctive yellow/cream livery? (When Glasgow trolleybus TBS21 turned up to tour the Cardiff system I was appalled to find it turned out in Halifax livery; didn't they know?)

Obviously, I had had to travel all the way to the city centre on it, hence my late arrival. Years later, as a parent myself, I understand the Pater's forceful argument in the subsequent discussion.

Must have been a bit of a bummer being a bus salesman. SGD was a Leyland demonstrator bought back from Glasgow (didn't they have access to one of their own?) leaving a hole where LA91 should have been. Cardiff went on to buy Fleetlines. It did buy some secondhand Atlanteans from Newcastle which spookily also wore yellow/cream garb. At least they knew what colour Glasgow buses were – or what I fondly imagined they were. About the same time, Rhondda borrowed 565 CRW, the Alexander Fleetline demo, and went on to buy Atlanteans. Ho hum . . . On the subject of having totally the wrong idea about liveries, I still remember my shock at seeing my first Barrow bus. Granted, I had enjoyed a few

Just look at the civic pride oozing from this. The AEC badge has been moved to the bottom of the radiator and replaced by the city coat of arms on a smart enamel badge. This graced the front of trolleybuses too (not the AEC badge, although some could rightly claim that). Then there's the rear wheel trims, a nice attention to detail, and the uncompromising fleetname: this is a Bradford bus, so there! It's nice the way the square-edged route numbers set off the fleetnumbers as well — makes you feel someone has thought about it. We have to forgive November 1963 vintage no.192 the crime of replacing trolleybuses on the splendid Crossflatts, Bingley, Bradford Moor (where was it?) routes; it was down to local politics. And the rebuilding of Forster Square, where it is seen in August 1966, but if the will had been there . . .
Photos by Roger Davies

Now here's a good one. Leeds is associated with AECs, but had a variety of Leylands, quite a lot of Daimlers and some Guys too. All in all a really representative municipal. Roe bodywork was favoured, but was kept on its toes by selective ordering of other bodies. The dear old Orion did its usual trick of looking good on an exposed-radiator Regent and simply vile on a tin-front Leyland, the 30-footers proving the point. But this chap, no.758, one of five from 1954, seen in February 1970, is a short Regent V with classic Leeds radiator cover and an Orion body. Now we all know of Roe's trademark staircase window, but how many knew of MCW's little rectangular one as seen here? It's entering the bus station with those flats in the background.

You could tell Huddersfield 'A' fleet buses by the swoopy cream at the front and the high fleetnumbers. No.582 in Northumberland Street has all this and is a bit obvious in being a trolleybus. Such things were getting rare by August 1966 and by the end of the year would be gone. Huddersfield continued with six-wheelers when it didn't legally need to, but if Cardiff's experience is anything to go by, it may have been connected with seating capacity too. Anyway there was no choice when this East Lancs-bodied Sunbeam MS2 was new in 1949. Huddersfield's trolleys were distinctive in having one big wing over the two rear axles.

pints of the sensational Hartley's bitter in Ulverston whilst watching *Kojak* on the TV, but it was a single-deck Fleetline and it was blue! C'mon, they were all dark red up there!

None of this is what I'm on about. Pre-announced trips to the city centre were common, mainly to visit Bud Morgan's. This Cardiff institution in the Castle Arcade (the Arcades were another Cardiff institution along with the sarsaparilla shop but that really is nothing whatever to do with this) was a model shop. And it was fantastic! Greens in Cowbridge Road was also super, but that meant getting off the motorbus from school where it popped out of a nondescript

side street, walking to the shop and catching a trolleybus home. Anyway, it was in Bud Morgan's that I found *British Bus Fleets 2 Yorkshire Municipals*. It was vast and 4s 6d as compared with the 3s for our South Wales BBF18. If you can't work all this out, you are too young to be reading this. And, what's more, it was just the Municipals; there was a separate book, BBF9, for Yorkshire Company Operators! This had to be paradise.

Discovering Leeds

You don't realise how barren your life is before you discover Leeds City Transport. Later, I applied for a

Halifax was another nice municipal mix, again majoring on AECs and Leylands, but with a goodly number of Daimlers. 'A' fleet No.115, a Roe-bodied CVG6, is in the bus station in August 1966. The livery was repeated on bus stop signs, some being green and others orange. It may have been to do with fare stages. They also sported an LT-like logo. This livery really made quite ordinary buses stand out and gave them presence. National Bus was criticised for getting rid of classic liveries, but the PTEs have arguably got more to answer for.

job with them in awe. Mind you, having a head office in Swinegate was a bit off-putting; still, NBC got to me first. As luck would have it, I had relatives in Bradford, and in 1965 a visit to them was mooted. A deal of pretty nifty salesmanship, probably indicating the fairer sex's addiction to such things, had converted my cousin to bus enthusiasm, so I set off, weighed down with BBFs 2 and 9 but with a light heart and many expectations.

A word about travel in those pre-motorway days. We went by car, a *Z-Cars*-style Ford Consul (I know they had Zephyrs but we're losing the youngsters by the bucketful now!). It was 225 miles, so entailed an overnight stay in Shrewsbury — the Red Lion (my father swore the big rendition of the beast on the hotel's front was pointing the other way in the morning). I did the 225 miles in under four hours and only checked the petrol gauge. Sorry guys, but BMMO homebrew single-decks creeping by in the night do nothing for me. Day two was when the excitement started. Threading through the

Manchester hinterland with plenty of North Western variety, including the amazing 'lowbridge' VALs, was something else. Then over the Pennines to Huddersfield. What a fleet, and passing through the town centre gave a tantalising taste of a huge variety of red/cream wonders. Although it was on its last legs, the trolleybus system was clearly one of Britain's finest. Heading for Bradford, the forlorn sight of disused wiring sweeping off to the right was heartrending. A quick whiz through pre-Terry Wogan Brighouse and the City of Bradford hove into view.

Well, not yet. Subsequent visits followed in 1966 and 1967. The 1967 trip included a side visit to London – I know it's a long way round, but it was pretty stunning to be there at the height of flower power. I bought a little bell. It's honestly depressing to think that buses that were running in London then, still are today. Leeds should still have Roe Regent Vs by right.

Memorable

The later visits were by train and my first journey was memorable. I had to travel to Manchester to be met by assorted cousins and be taken by train on to Bradford. Nearing Manchester, the view over Mersey Square in Stockport was unbelievable. The local corporation had a really smart red/cream traditional fleet. I had a book, *The Boys' Bumper Book Of Trains* or somesuch. One drawing featured some train or other passing under a bridge graced by a splendid trolleybus in Stockport livery. Maybe the artist thought it would have been a good idea too! Years later, after a terrorist attack on a coach, luggage lockers were being checked as vehicles on coach work entered the square. The security folks insisted on checking the boot of Trent's vehicle on the Manchester-Derby run. It was a double-deck ECW Fleetline.

We walked from Manchester Piccadilly station down a main thoroughfare. There were billions of red buses, all with huge four-figure fleetnumbers in big thin red figures on the back. They had neat little gold ones on the front too. I tried to memorise as many as possible to refer back to in BBF6. And what variety; they may all have been red, but no two seemed the same. Then at the end of the street was a bus station absolutely full of green Salford buses! Wasn't that somewhere else? Why did they have their bus station in Manchester?

Then to Bradford. Ah, Bradford. I'm sure current residents will forgive me when I say the city was a bit grim in the 1960s. It was a revelation as refurbishment revealed just what a beautiful colour the stone buildings really were; in the 1960s they were black. It was a masterstroke to paint the buses bright blue/cream; they cheered up the scene and gave the city identity. (Pause for moan about the completely inappropriate use of corporate identity on buses.) Now look, 30ft front-entrance Orion-bodied Regent Vs were company buses. Rhondda had hordes that belted off to Maerdy and Treorchy and the like. Bradford had hordes (definition of 'hordes' – 120) that went to Wrose, Heaton and Bradford Moor. They had wonderful exhaust brakes and the city was alive with their screams and roars. I know it was a bit raucous what with trolleybuses and that, but they were lovely. They had 'Bus Stopping' signs inside, very continental, and huge square-edged route numbers. They were very Bradford.

Sleek

There were lots of other buses too including Leyland-bodied Leylands. Company buses or what? There were two distinct batches, 554-73 which were quite old-looking and, a year newer, 41-65 with sleek Farington-type bodies. What a difference a year makes. Except no.564 which had had the beading removed from above the front upper deck windows so looked like a Farington. Phew, sorry, getting a bit heavy there. All these seemed to be in service, whilst assortments of other buses gathered dust at Thornbury Works. (If I mention this enough, someone may explain it!) My relatives lived on Cleckheaton Road on the 85 to Oakenshaw, just over the city boundary. Bankfoot depot did the honours and mainly turned out Leylands from the earlier batch. From the city, the poor things would grind up miles of Manchester Road until hitting the flat at Odsal Top for about 50 yards before zooming down to Oakenshaw. OK, on the return they whizzed down quite a way, but, boy, did those buses work! I was inordinately jealous that no.566 had bumped into my cousin's bedroom in a fog. Sometimes a Regent V appeared, although these were usually on the City Circle. Bankfoot had the first 15, which were the nicest, having no opening front vents and looking a little wider. I don't suppose I'll ever get Michael Dryhurst waxing lyrical about Orions like he does about four- and five-bays! There were 25 ex-London RTs, which didn't look quite right somehow. Maybe

Yorkshire Woollen provided a super mix of buses on its share of the 66, which only ran to Dewsbury, so was called 65. Got it? Nasty Weymann-bodied Lowlanders mixed with Orion forward-entrance PD3s (but not similar Regent Vs) and later with Alexander-bodied Fleetlines and Atlanteans that also introduced a cream stripe. Pride of place must go to no.699 (HD 8553) and its five sisters, rebodied by Roe in 1963 on PS2 chassis dating back to 1951. These really threw me. It's in Chester Street, Bradford before commencing its climb back up to Odsal Top.

LT keeps some buses for a long time, but even some of its favourites got kicked out quite soon. Before the Regent Vs there were to-die-for Regent IIIs with Weymann bodies, followed by some with East Lancs bodies spoiled by Birmingham-style tin fronts. Thankfully, a rare occurrence.

Now you may be aware that there were trolleybuses. They were just about everywhere and, cutting across the suburbs, almost every main road you crossed was wired. There were still lengthy sections of depot wiring and the 40-42 Saltaire, Shipley, Greengates group was isolated from the rest of the system apart from such wiring. With the city being so hilly, it was ideal ground for them and they climbed the steep streets effortlessly. The system was very impressive and not at all run-'down' and there seemed no reason to get rid of it. They just quietly got on with the job. Boring, but important. In fact, a fluorescent lighting, platform door equipped trolleybus with bright Formica interior was a much

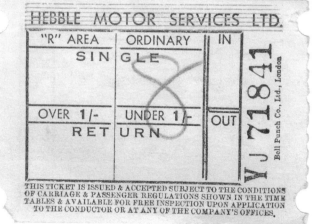

HEBBLE MOTOR SERVICES LTD.

"R" AREA	ORDINARY	IN
SINGLE		
OVER 1/-	UNDER 1/-	OUT
RETURN		

YJ 71841   Bell Punch Co., Ltd., London

THIS TICKET IS ISSUED & ACCEPTED SUBJECT TO THE CONDITIONS OF CARRIAGE & PASSENGER REGULATIONS SHOWN IN THE TIME TABLES & AVAILABLE FOR FREE INSPECTION UPON APPLICATION TO THE CONDUCTOR OR AT ANY OF THE COMPANY'S OFFICES.

better bet for retaining customer loyalty than the rather dull Leylands.

Clearly, Bradford had some pull. A joint service, the 72, was run with the mighty Leeds City Transport to that city. At the time LCT was wedded to rear entrances but all BCT's finest had front doors. This'll confuse the punters, says someone (long before the term punter was used in such a way), so LCT bought five forward-entrance CVG6/30s just for the 72! Some going by smaller BCT!

Leeds was amazing. On my first visit I stood in the Headrow and could not believe the endless rows of green buses. By then the lighter shade was around the bottom-deck widows the rest being dark apart from the silver bonnet covers. Neither was a particularly nice greens, but they worked together and with the smart fleetname just exuded professionalism and confidence. You took one look at its buses and you just knew this was some city! The reversal of livery for driver-only buses

a la Manchester was sheer genius. And if you liked AECs this was some form of Nirvana. I allowed myself the treat of liking the 30ft Orions best; the Roes were somehow just too neat for their own good. The same could most certainly not be said of their PD3s; the Orions were vile. Such was the power of variety. And they had one of my favourite destinations: 'South Accommodation Road Circular'.

Mess

I go back to Leeds sometimes for a withdrawn busmen's reunion lunch. It's a mess, buses in all sorts of liveries and the increasingly dominant one the same in Penzance, Glasgow and Leicester, about as relevant as an ashtray on a motorcycle. Oh, and Sheffield. 1960s-style civic pride, where the two cities vied to be the capital of Yorkshire, a battle also fought with shiny new state-of-the-art offerings in the halls of the annual bus and coach exhibition (then at Earls Court,, would never have allowed that.

A walk to Odsal Top brought access to route 64, the Bradford-Huddersfield service jointly run by the two corporations and Hebble. Huddersfield was one of those Yorkshire oddities with a Joint Committee. Halifax was too, Todmorden was all one and Sheffield had three! Now let's not get bogged down here. In simple terms, the railways had got all mixed up in it and, in effect, the territorial company operations around these places were provided by a joint committee or 'B' fleet but the buses were all one fleet. This meant very large operating areas. In Huddersfield you could tell which was which by the livery and fleetnumber. It had been a giveaway when the Corporation 'A' fleet buses were trolleybuses, but this was changing. The Corporation buses had cream swoops on the front - I'm not a swoop man myself – whilst the joint 'B' fleet buses were in the rather

fetching red with three cream bands; I thought this livery was a classic. The corporation buses were numbered from 400 up, the joint ones being lower numbers. Ever the adventurer, I had noted in BBF9 a fleet called County Motors of Lepton. Here in Lord Street, terminus of the 64, was a dinky little Guy-bodied Guy Arab LUF, no.6 in the joint fleet, proclaiming 'Lepton'. Off we set. Off to Lepton, up a hill affording a splendid view of County's depot as it disappeared into the distance on a different road. Frantic ringing of the bell, this being a piece of wooden bole set in a trough stretching the length of the bus, finally effected our escape. We should have caught a 73 trolleybus to Waterloo. Obvious really.

Halifax was a different do all together. There wasn't a through service until 1971, so a change at Hebden Bridge and an involvement with Todmorden was necessary. I remember peering tentatively into Todmorden's depot and being invited in by an amiable member of staff. Makes a lasting impression; I always liked Tod. Anyway, what can you say about Halifax? The green, orange and cream livery, common to both 'A' and 'B' fleets, was sensational; you just couldn't miss them and the fleet was hugely varied. They even had Royal Tiger Worldmasters! They really did seem like a company operator and, in due course, they really with, the Calderdale episode involving Todmorden and Hebble. But this is a long way off. It is still remembered as an operator of huge charisma, and bus enthusiasts would always rise to the famous and frequent criticism of the town with a 'Yes, but what about those buses!' Halifax is the poorer without them.

I mentioned BBF9, *Yorkshire Company Operators*, and what a splendid bunch they were. I've saved this bit up because it's remarkable and makes you realise what we are missing now. My relatives lived on BCT's

85 which ran every half hour, so it was just as well that this wasn't all. There was also the 65/66, which, probably due to some extension of city boundaries in the past, was allowed to pick up and set down on Cleckheaton Road. So we could use that. It was run – wait for it – jointly by Yorkshire Woollen, Yorkshire Traction and Sheffield Transport! Can you imagine travelling on another corporation's bus locally in a city 30 miles away? Stunning. Mind you, it was part of Sheffield's third fleet, the 'C' fleet that ran miles out of the city, reaching such wonders as Manchester, Gainsborough, Castleton and Buxton. Er, hang on, some of those may have been 'B' fleet routes – anyway, what an operator! The 66 was the through route to Sheffield taking no less than 2hr 50min via Dewsbury and Barnsley. It was hourly even on Sunday afternoons. Interestingly, Bradford's route 66 to Norwood Green ran quite near and Sheffield had

Like many major cities, Bradford enjoyed the service of various company operators, depending on which side of the city you were. North was the preserve of West Yorkshire and also of Samuel Ledgard, which, along with West Yorkshire, features in Alan Bennett monologues. This was a whole new concept to me, a private operator providing a company operator style of network. Sammy's blue/grey buses were quite widespread and in places like Otley were dominant. The fleet was a fabulous mix of some new and many prudent secondhand purchases. RTs and RLHs (a personal favourite) mixed with ex-South Wales Regent Vs (which later passed to West Yorkshire, imagine that!) and ex-Bristol ECW PD2s. The Bradford ice-rink was the scene of my discovery that I couldn't skate but five-year olds were brilliant. However, they couldn't possibly know that in front, in Chester Street, was this delight, GDK 405 an ex-Rochdale East Lancs-bodied Regent III of 1948. Sammy's looked the part except for fleetnumbers.

another 66, the Stocksbridge town service. Gosh, we took all this for granted! Tracky also ran through, but Woollen only went to Dewsbury and called it the 65. Let me pass on a secret. In those days, inter-company revenue balancing was regarded as the cornerstone of company finance. Every penny had to be properly apportioned and huge departments existed for this vital function. On these routes, there was obviously complex revenue apportionment and on the through buses you had to rebook at Barnsley. The competition authorities have seen that off today — it's not in the public interest to have joint operation.

More tasteful

Back to more tasteful things. Sheffield's usual offerings were Roe- or ECW- (I kid you not) bodied PD2s with high-backed seating and platform doors that were rather luxurious. Tracky favoured forward-entrance NCME-bodied PD3s with sliding doors. I remember being clouted by one of these as it slid shut when we came to a halt on the downhill return from town. It was heavy.

Now Woollen may not have had it in livery stakes — they were a bit of a drab red — but boy did they have buses! They were beyond me. I could handle rebodied wartime Guys, some hailing from M&D, but PS Tigers rebodied as deckers was too much. The bulk had rear-entrance Orions and, bless them, they struggled up the hills and whizzed down them like good 'uns, but there were six absolute gems. These had Roe forward-entrance bodies but still HD-plus-four-number registrations. I just couldn't come to terms with their fluorescent lights, Formica and doors and such old registrations! There was clearly no concern for the punters' confusion over door positions on these routes!

Each company had its own main area: Tracky's was Barnsley and Woollen was Dewsbury. Woollen also had hordes of forward- entrance Orion Regent Vs

(hordes in this case is 34) but I never saw one outside Dewsbury. They were more Bradford than Rhondda in this respect. And others. Then there was Hebble. There's a whole tale to tell about company operators having a toe-hold in municipals' urban areas but Hebble was the toe-hold to end them all! It really didn't have an area of its own and it was pretty bright of BET to invent it. I've heard it described as the 'C' fleet Halifax didn't have! All over the place you'd find Hebble buses in their rather nice shade of BET red with cream lower-deck window surrounds, always a pleasing layout, going about their mainly urban business. It was just plain clever! I remember a journey on my favourite Hebble, and indeed one of my all-time favourite buses, Regent V no.316, on a 64. We made very slow progress. We waited at junctions for an age. Finally alighting at Odsal, I looked in the cab. The driver must have been 106 if he was a day. Things got a bit rough at the end, and at the final demise West Yorkshire took over the workings on the 64. Sorry, but an FS Lodekka isn't on the same planet as a Regent V.

My Yorkshire visit in 1966 took place immediately after my O-level results and was designed to prove life existed after them. It was also after the purchase of The Beatles *Revolver* probably the best album ever. I recall with fondness a trip to some stretch of the River Aire by Sammy Ledgard bus and hearing the strains of 'And Your Bird Can Sing' emitting from a remote farmhouse. I remembered this, so, after my daughter's GCSEs, we went to Cork. Somehow, Wright-bodied Volvos don't measure up . . . **CB**